A DORSET UTOPIA

The Little Commonwealth and Homer Lane

JUDITH STINTON

BLACK DOG BOOKS

First published in England 2005
by Black Dog Books
104 Trinity Street, Norwich, Norfolk, NR2 2BJ.

A CIP record of this book is available from the British Library.

ISBN 0-9528839-4-5

Typeset in 12 point Times

Printed in Great Britain
by Biddles Ltd., *www.biddles.co.uk.*

Frontispiece - Homer Lane with two girl citizens.

For
Harriet Smedley

Acknowledgements

Many people have helped in the making of this book. First of all, 1 would like to thank Hugh Jaques, the county archivist, his staff at Dorset Record Office - especially Peter Irvine - and the owner of the Little Commonwealth archive deposited there. I would also like to thank Clare Fleck and the owners of the Knebworth House archive; Malcolm Taylor of the English Folk Dance & Song Society; Brian Ryder, University of Reading; Pat Styles, the Scout Association; the staff of the Institute of Education, the British Library, the Public Record Office, the Home Office Library, the Dorset County Museum (especially the then curator, Richard de Peyer), and Warwick Modern Records Centre. David Brown, Sylvia Coffin, Abi Cox, Max Hebditch, John and Sara Hudston, Gill King, Martin Lascelles, Mike and Sheila Leaman, Frances Nicholson, Zoe Readhead and Rayner Unwin have all helped in different ways.

I would particularly like to thank Colin Ward who, along with Alistair Wilson, went to a great deal of trouble to find a tape of the Radio 4 programme on Lane; and also Bryn Purdy, with whom 1 have had a lively and productive correspondence. My publisher Peter Tolhurst has once again been very supportive. And I am grateful to Brother Philip Bartholomew and Brother Reginald of the Society of Saint Francis, Hilfield.

Finally I would like to thank Craig Fees, archivist of the Planned Environment Therapy Trust, and his staff for their kindness and interest. I have had many conversations about Homer Lane with Craig Fees, who has provided a different and valuable perspective on this fascinating man.

Illustrations
The author is most grateful to the following:
Bridgeman Art Library, front cover; Dorset County Museum, nos 2-4, 24, 43; Dorset Record Office, nos 5, 12, 18, 19, 22, 31-33; English Folk Song & Dance Society, nos 35 & 36; Hilfield Friary Archive, nos 6, 7, 20, 21, 23, 26-28, 30; F.R.Hoare, no 11; F.Kennard, no 10; Lyme Regis Museum, no 42; Planned Environment Therapy Trust, frontispiece & nos 14-17, 39, 40; Scout Association, no 9.

To comply with the requirements of the Data Protection Act, citizens' names have been changed.

Contents

I wander thro' each charter'd street,
Near where the charter'd Thames does flow
And mark in every face I meet
Marks of weakness, marks of woe.

In every cry of every Man,
In every Infants cry of fear,
In every voice; in every ban,
The mind-forg'd manacles I hear...

From 'London' by William Blake (*Songs of Experience*, 1794)

Foreword

Graham Greene once wrote a story about a man who was killed when he was sat on by a pig. Such a ridiculous fate would render the rest of the man's life unmemorable, however eventful it might really have been.

Few people, other than professional child care workers, now remember Homer Lane. Those who do remember his inglorious end. Lane's life was full of incident: he lived whole-heartedly, heedless of what this might do to his health and his reputation. Central to this life were his years at the Little Commonwealth in deepest Dorset, where he led a unique experiment in self-government with boys and girls from the city slums, children mostly with criminal records. It was an experiment that would seem radical even today.

The Little Commonwealth closed prematurely after some of the girls made accusations against Lane. Lane was almost certainly innocent of the charges, but they ruined his career and have shadowed accounts of his remarkable achievements with troubled children.

This book is an attempt to recreate the Little Commonwealth years - as far as possible from the children's viewpoint - and to return Lane's work to the centre of the debate on the treatment of young offenders.

Judith Stinton

1. Extract from the 1919 edition of the 1" Ordinance Survey map showing the Little Commonwealth.

1
The Deptford Terror

Into Tower Bridge Police Court went three girls, all charged with theft. They were strikingly light-fingered thieves. The eldest, fifteen year old Ellen Stanley, could lift a bale of cloth from a draper's counter and conceal it under her apron without being noticed. For months the police had been watching them, even hiring a special detective to catch them. Now at last Ellen had been caught and charged, along with Mary Derbyshire and Annie Scott, her two younger accomplices.

They did not come quietly. Struggling, swearing and shouting in backslang, they were hauled into the courtroom. Their school records were read to the court; the girls were sulky and unrepentant. When Annie caught sight of her sobbing mother, she too began to cry, until one of the other girls whispered stagily, 'Don't be a fool. Stare 'em out'. Things were not going well.

But the girls were more fortunate than they realised. The magistrate hearing the case was Cecil Chapman, a man much concerned with alternative methods of sentencing young delinquents. And observing the proceedings in court was a big sandy-haired American called Homer Lane. He was there to select suitable children for an experimental institution in the remote Dorset countryside at Flowers Farm, Batcombe. This was to be called 'The Little Commonwealth'.

At first sight the girls, (Lane wrote) were 'certainly not very promising material', though he had been struck by their behaviour when they were finally caught. 'When the girls were arrested in the act of secreting some stolen articles, one of them had said: "I'll come along and own up if you'll let that girl go," indicating a fourth and younger member of the group. At this point I determined to try to get these girls for the Commonwealth.' Lane saw the girls' thieving as a healthy and legitimate reaction to their surroundings and upbringing. He seemed to relish their bad behaviour. Chapman also thought them ideal. They were intelligent, he said, yet at the same time 'challengingly difficult to deal with'. He made the decision to refer them, despite the overwhelming opposition of the rest of the Court.

Ellen, Mary and Annie were remanded in custody for a week whilst their futures were resolved. The Little Commonwealth had not yet received a Home Office licence, so children could only be placed there - rather than in a remand home - with their parents' consent.

A week later, Lane went to collect them. He refused to use handcuffs, or the police matron and two constables who had been assigned to help him. Instead he sent one girl off to find a taxi cab while he waited with the other two. At Paddington Station he himself went to buy the tickets, leaving the girls to buy newspapers to read on the train. As Lane recalled, he gave them 'abundant opportunity to escape' and they made no attempt to take it. 'Thus their first contact with the Commonwealth was that of responsibility and confidence.'

The three children were known, Lane was to say, as 'The Terror of

2. Evershot Station c.1905.

3. Batcombe Down.

Deptford'. They came from the small impoverished streets between dockyard and creek and would scarcely have given a thought to the world beyond the narrow alleyways and the looping River Thames. To them, Dorset must have seemed as distant as any penal colony: Van Diemen's Land could have been their fate only sixty years before. The day of their journey was 9 July, 1913, in the high summer, so it was probably still light when they reached Evershot Station, one of the many stops on the cross-country line between Bristol and Weymouth. The station was actually at Holywell, some distance from the estate village of Evershot, and from the great house and deer park of Melbury Sampford.

It was an even greater distance from Flowers Farm. Leaving the station, they would have crossed Long Ash Lane, a part of the trunk road linking Dorset and Somerset, but still described in 1922 as 'a lovely, grass-grown straight track filled with eternal peace'. They climbed the long steep rise of Batcombe Hill. Now they were out in the wilds. Batcombe Down lay ahead of them, with its frugal covering of

4. Telegraph Hill, looking towards Dogbury Hill, by Hermann Lea, 1913.

bracken, bramble and heather. Directly below Batcombe Church was visible, pinnacled against the hills. Beyond it were the village's scanty attractions: the line of strung-out cottages, the old poorhouse and the scattering of parish farms.

The road - the dusty track - on which they travelled was a borderland: the edge of the chalklands is to its south. Northwards are the green and watery fields of the Blackmore Vale, stretching as far as the eye can see to an expansive blue horizon. The road hairpins sharply down Telegraph Hill, to join the Sherborne road on through Minterne and the badlands of Lyons Gate.

Just before Telegraph Hill, though, is a track which drops almost vertically downwards. It plunges through a dense pine tunnel, banked in dark green ferns. There beneath the woods lies Flowers Farm, the place selected as the girls' new home.

In less than a day they had journeyed from the cramped and lively, grimy and low-lying streets of London to the uncanny silences of the overhanging woods, the bewildering isolation of an unaccustomed country.

One girl had arrived before them, on 27 June. She was Vera Cooke, aged sixteen, also from London. Vera was a private referral, who had been sent there by her parents. (Voluntary cases could be referred without being charged before a magistrate.) She had already run away from two other institutions. She was said to be of 'limited mental capacity' and her offence was described as 'incorrigibility', meaning that she was 'beyond correction, reform or alteration'.

Lane was to claim that he began with girls because he believed they would settle in more easily. He watched the process closely. So did the press: this social experiment already had a certain celebrity. According to the *Daily Express*, the girls arrived 'in the tears and rags of the mean streets'. At their first meal, asked whether they would prefer white bread or brown, they simply replied "It doesn't matter". They constantly sought each other's opinions and seemed much overawed by their surroundings. When required to make a list of the clothes they needed the *Express* said that 'every one of them plumped for corsets', although these were 'quietly discarded' when the girls sensed their housemother did not approve.

Within a week they apparently adapted themselves well and surprisingly quickly, judging by a postcard sent by one of the girls to the institution's London office:

'Just a few lines to you ow a enjoy the train ride from London to Evershot, and I enjoy my ride round London. It was a fine ride. I like it out he very much. I want a new pair of working boots.'

The girls 'naturally' began to help with the housework, assisting their housemother Mrs Beth Jones. Both she and Lane were somewhat apprehensive about the effects of the arrival of boys; Mrs Jones feared what seemed to her to be the inevitable and disastrous results of co-education, while Lane was aware that the boys would shatter the peace. Not that he minded too much: 'I knew that our peace was the peace of stagnation and that boys were less apt than girls to be influenced by the beauties of nature, the lovely hills and flowers and spaces of the country, and there would probably be the necessity for the introduction of some form of authority to limit the scope of their experiments.'

After about two weeks the boys appeared. Firstly, there was Will Sharp, 'ex-bad boy of Hoxton', Ted Dalston, Robert Brewer, Harry Billen and then a day later, Jim O'Donnell. Lane and the girls walked to meet them at Evershot. The boys alighted from the train, 'swaggering and laughing boisterously, smoking cigarettes, dirty and unkempt'. So Lane put it, and newspaper reports adopt much the same tone, as if football hooligans had invaded a dolls' tea party. The four girls had become accustomed to the countryside. Now they had to get used to the boys.

Back at Flowers Farm the girls had prepared a special tea and decorated the dining-room. The boys were given a separate table, with flowers and the best of the cakes. The meal passed 'without incident', though the boys disappeared immediately after it - like tom cats - to explore their strange new territory. They returned late in the evening with red-stained mouths. They had been raiding the strawberry beds.

The order of the household, tentative and new-found as it had been, was now completely upset. The boys made no contribution to the housework. They regarded washing themselves as 'swanky'. They were rowdy at night. The overwhelming silence of the countryside frightened them - a silence broken only by the throaty barking of a fox, or a stag's belling, or the call of some unidentifiable bird. Unnerved, they would move their beds into another boy's room and 'sleep double'. Beth Jones had thought that bringing an unruly bunch of boys and girls together in early adolescence was bound to end in disaster. She seemed at first to be vindicated, as one boy and girl promptly paired off. The arrangement, though, did not last long. The disillusioned girl soon retreated back from the boys' table, disgusted by the slurping sounds of soup-drinking. The boys, in their turn, were contemptuous of the chattering girls.

The boys had shattered the peace, and Homer Lane refused to do anything about it. He was not, he said, a policeman. Like the boys, he too would do whatever he liked: smash windows, laze about, steal strawberries. To the amazement of the girls, and of his assistants Mr and Mrs Jones, he left the children to sort things out for themselves.

2
The Little Commonwealth

At the end of July 1913, a representative of the *Dorset County Chronicle* paid a visit to the recently-opened Commonwealth. His resulting article filled several columns of the newspaper. It began:

'The celebrity attained by Plato's "Republic", Sir Thomas More's "Utopia", and Lord Bacon's "New Atlantis" reminds us of the interest taken in all ages in sociological and governmental experiments. One such experiment is now being tried at Batcombe, in the green heart of Dorset, "far from the madding crowd's ignoble strife", and although it is but on a small scale as yet...it is justly attracting the attention of thoughtful people all over the country, especially those interested in the treatment of juvenile crime, the correction of early faults and the development and due direction of youthful character. Of late years there has been a marked change in public sentiment on this subject and in the resultant legal attitude

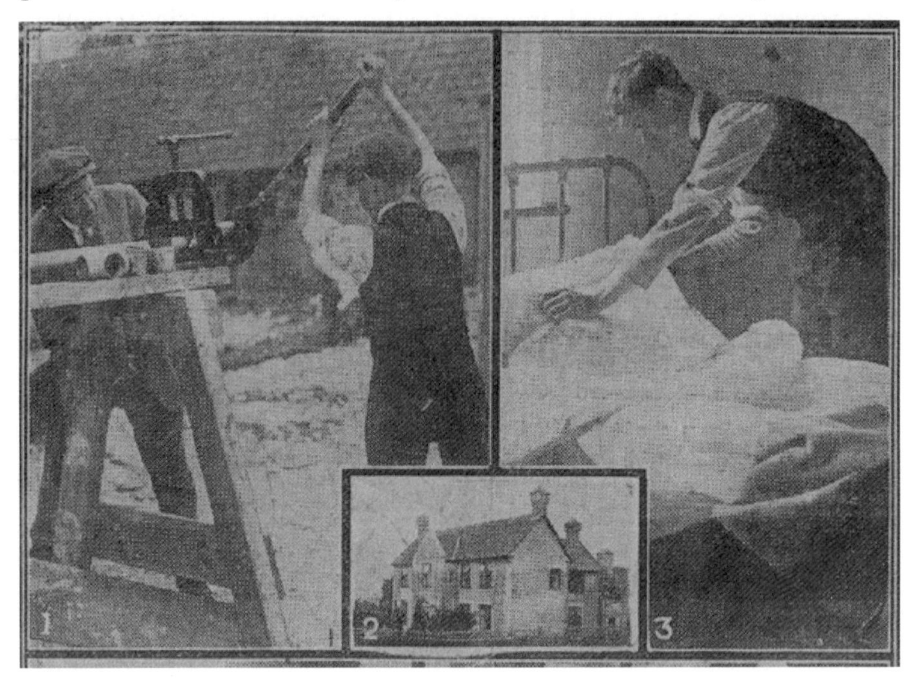

5. 'Juvenile Republic in Dorset'.
5.1. 'A first lesson in plumbing'. 5.2. Flowers Farm. 5.3. 'Making his bed'.

towards it. It is now recognised that much which used to be called "crime" among the rising generation, especially in the slums of our great cities, is rather the result of such a combination of evil heredity and prejudicial environment as largely to reduce the moral culpability of the young offender. To pick him out of his unfavourable circumstances, to give him a better start in "fresh woods and pastures new" under the wholesome influences of Mother Nature and wise and kindly supervision - herein apparently lies the secret of just amelioration.'

The reporter interviewed Homer Lane and George Montagu, founder of the Little Commonwealth and nephew and heir of the eighth Earl of Sandwich (he became the ninth Earl in 1916). The interview took place in Flowers Farmhouse, amidst the building works and the lively presence of about a dozen 'citizens', as the children were called. George Montagu explained their plans. The farmhouse, to which an extra storey had been already added, was set in 190 acres of land. The landowner, Lord Sandwich, had leased farmhouse and land to the enterprise for twenty-one years. Two new cottages, thatched and red-brick, were being built by R.G.Spiller of Sherborne and Chard. Each would house around ten to fifteen children, under the care of a house-parent. The community was expected to grow quickly and it was hoped eventually to have as many as a hundred children.

At the far end of the courtyard to the rear of the farmhouse, buildings were being converted into a shop, where citizens would buy and sell their own stores. There would be a laundry, and a barn was to be turned into an assembly room. The less skilled construction work was being done by the citizens themselves, who were building walls and roads. They had already erected a pumping-engine and

6. Flowers Farm, with Mr & Mrs Jones.

7. Building the Pumping House.

plant, now entirely under the charge of a fourteen year old citizen, 'Engineer Harry'.

At this point in the interview, Lane took over. 'The idea...is to give the boys and girls definite responsibility, and to encourage them to perfect themselves in it. On the practical and industrial side this place will really be a technical school, where useful crafts will be carefully and thoroughly taught, and will be largely self-contained and self-supporting...' Citizens would learn how to bake bread, make and mend their own clothes and repair their own boots. Girls would do the sewing, and boys the tailoring. There was an established daily routine with breakfast at 7.30 am, dinner at 12 noon, tea at 5pm and a light supper at 8pm. Between tea and supper there was time for 'recreation and amusement'.

As well as looking after themselves, citizens were to be responsible for making laws. Rules would be drawn up on an ad hoc basis as the necessity arose. Adults would attend meetings only to advise.

Each citizen would have a job - the boys in the stables or out on the farm, the girls in the house. They were paid not in real money but an equivalent amount in aluminium tokens. These they could spend at the shop, though they were encouraged to build up a 'nest-egg' for when they left. (They could not be spent in any other place, thereby removing at least one temptation.) Wages tallied with current rates. As well as paying for food, clothes, rent and taxes, citizens eventually had to pay into a health insurance scheme. Wages were increased during the course of the War by a penny ha'penny an hour to keep pace with outside pay and prices. There were taxes to be paid, and board and lodgings. Lane explained the Commonwealth's economic ethos in more detail :

'The assumption is that the committee who are the owners of the property wish to develop it; and we are living here as a contracting party to carry out that development. We are to improve the property; and the committee, instead of, say, buying bread and sending it down here to support the community, will pay the community for the work they do, and with that money the community can buy their own bread. Thus we shall have what we earn.'

Lane spoke with confidence and optimism. The Little Commonwealth: with its 'shining ideals, gleaming hope, and great possibilities', as the *Chronicle* concluded, had now really begun.

3
Foundations

The idea of a self-governing community, as George Montagu had pointed out in his interview with the *Chronicle*, was not entirely new. He referred vaguely - 'speaking from memory' - to schemes in the sixteenth and eighteenth centuries in Germany and Scotland. In England, a school near Birmingham had been started by the father of Rowland Hill, creator of the penny post. However, the community's most obvious and direct precursor was the George Junior Republic in Freeville, New York State. This self-governing institution opened in 1890, with a constitution modelled on that of the United States. It had its own courts, police, prison and punishments and reflected the status quo. The Little Commonwealth, although outwardly similar, was to develop self-government more democratically and organically, shaped more by collective decisions than by any structure imposed upon it.

George Charles Montagu had been Member of Parliament for South Huntingdonshire from 1900-1906. His home at Hinchingbrooke in Huntingdon had once been the seat of Oliver Cromwell's family - an appropriate background for the founder of a 'Little Commonwealth'.

Montagu was no impractical idealist. He concerned himself greatly with juvenile delinquency, was a member of the Borstal Committee, and went to visit the George Republic. In October 1911 he declared his intention to open a similar institution in England, to be called the Citizen Boys' Guild, with a few boys aged from sixteen to eighteen, selected from the courts of the larger towns. For Montagu, as for Homer Lane, the faults of delinquent boys were often 'very good qualities run wild'.

In December 1911, Montagu spoke again of his plans during the annual meeting of the Penal Reform League, at which he explained that he would have to begin his republic with boys alone, 'to avoid the antagonism of the Home Office'. His audience, however, contained 'some eminent suffragettes'. Two of them, Lady Constance Lytton and Miss Sylvia Pankhurst, 'moved that such an enterprise would be unsatisfactory if girls and women were left out', as the *British Journal*

8. Duchess of Marlborough.

of Nursing reported on 16 December, 1911. Thereafter, even though newspaper reports continued to call the proposed institution a 'Boys' Republic' or even a 'Bad Boys' Utopia', Montagu's many fund-raising speeches included plans for girls as well as boys. Girls were to have equal rights with boys, they would be able to vote (which they could not do in the world outside) and they would also be encouraged to garden, using an 'intensive culture on the French system'. Boys would learn to cook. Only in their sleeping arrangements would they be segregated; boys and girls would sleep in separate cottages which they would have to build for themselves.

Montagu worked tirelessly to promote his scheme, appealing to many (mainly metropolitan) meetings. His cause soon became a modish one. As well as Asquiths and Astors, it attracted journalists like Harold Child of the *Times*; writers like John Galsworthy and Desmond MacCarthy; actor-manager Herbert Beerbohm Tree; Mary Neal, folk-dance revivalist; social reformers Emmeline and Frederick Pethrick-Lawrence; along with bishops, teachers and prison officers. The story was reported by newspapers all over the world.

In June 1912 'a crowded and fashionable gathering' came together at Sunderland House to hear Earl Grey inaugurate the new community. So many people attended that an overflow meeting had to be arranged, and 'everyone stayed for tea'. The fashionable crowds were there at the invitation of Consuelo, Duchess of Marlborough, who proved a generous donor to the scheme, providing £450 towards the costs of a girls' cottage. For publicity purposes, though, she was herself something of a distraction. An American heiress, she was separated from her husband, and had dedicated herself to social causes. Contemporary accounts of the event are much taken up with photographs and descriptions of her clothing. (The Duchess was sporting a white dress and a large, dark hat.)

The Duchess of Marlborough became one of the twelve members of the Commonwealth's General Committee, which also included Bertram Brooke, the 'Rajah of Sarawak', and Thomas Mott Osborne, President of the George Junior Republic Association and Governor of Sing Sing Prison. Montagu became Chairman of the Executive, and his uncle was Chairman of the General Committee until his death in 1916, when Lord Victor Lytton took his place. Montagu's wife, Alberta, and the magistrate Cecil Chapman were the other founder members of the Executive Committee, to be joined by banker Otto Beit, Bertram

Hawker of the Montessori Society and Sir Matthew Nathan. The President was Earl Grey.

The newspapers were in the main enthusiastic, if somewhat facetious, about the Little Commonwealth, although there was much anti-American feeling about its prototype. This was one of the reasons why it was decided not to call the institution a republic. 'Only those methods which harmonize with English life and English traditions' would be applied. Whatever the labels used, Lane later observed that English children took to self-government more readily than their American counterparts.

The amount needed to begin the project was about £15,000. Flowers Farm was leased from Montagu's uncle for an annual peppercorn rent of £140. Reports described the building as 'a roomy house built substantially of stone in 1888 by the Paulett family, whose familiar arms, three swords with their points meeting, are scuptured on a stone escutcheon in the front'. Montagu soon succeeded in raising the money. In those prosperous, pre-war Edwardian days, it was comparatively easy. Social reform was in the air, and many an altruistic scheme was being launched.

Sir Robert Baden-Powell had already begun a Boy Scout farm at Buckhurst Place, outside Wadhurst in Sussex, in a mansion ('a most imposing edifice') which had been built as a private mental hospital. There, forty-five Scouts were grouped in patrols, and each patrol was given a specific duty for a month - 'on animals' or 'on land'. Other agricultural subjects were taught in the evenings. The aim was to train boys for farming at home or 'in the Dominions' where, 'turned loose' with axe and bag of wheat, they could build for themselves a 'thriving homestead'.

Baden-Powell said that the school would 'form a community somewhat on the lines of the Boys' Republics', though the Scouts were not delinquent. At Buckhurst Farm, he said, 'the boy comes first'. The family unit was the patrol, in which decisions were taken, and the Scouts elected the farm's Mayor, Council and Court of Honour. Homer Lane's biographer, David Wills, thought Baden-Powell's patrol system an inspired idea, as 'the young male adolescent loves to be one of a

9. Boy Scout Farm, Buckhurst Place, Sussex.

gang following devotedly a revered and respected leader'. Contemporary Scouting newspapers announced that the scheme had been an unqualified success, cut short only by the seemingly endless First World War. Buckhurst Farm closed in 1916 after the general call-up of eighteen year olds made it impossible to continue.

Apart from a training colony for the reformation of young prostitutes run by M.L. Shaw in Newbury, the other major children's community active in the Great War was at Sysonby House, Riverside Village, Melton Mowbray, set up by the Fellowship of Reconciliation. Like the Little Commonwealth, it took adolescent delinquents, mostly from London. The superintendent F. Russell Hoare said that Riverside was meant to help children 'whom for some reason or other nobody else will touch': boys and girls who had been labelled as 'helpless, unhelpable, hopeless'. Hoare was an anarchist by temperament, who had no desire to turn out good 'citizens', but rather rebels - individuals capable of thinking for themselves. He noted how children's faces changed as 'the mask drops away' when they came to know themselves as individuals. Like Lane, Hoare relied on the strength of his own personality to carry out his work. He rejected all forms of government, including self-government in which he detected '"the hidden hand" of the adult manipulator, quite a different person from the adult participator.'

Hoare also rejected all forms of punishment, which he saw as expressions of 'the power of fear'. Like Lane he regarded love as being of the greatest importance: '...if you ask me whether I think that it is possible to love in this way any and every wretched warped creature that comes to you for help, whether, conversely, every one has something lovable in them if you could only find it, I can only say that in fact I have found that when I have been brought into close contact with such people, and when I have thrown myself unreservedly into their lives, I have loved them like that...' The strongest love, Hoare believed, often showed itself in 'standing by', in witholding from action.

10. Sysonby House, Riverside Village, Melton Mowbray.

Perceptively, Hoare pointed out that 'emotional instability' had never been confined to adolescents. Adults also had to understand what they could and could not do - they too had to know themselves and be themselves if they were to be of any use in dealing with adolescents. In particular they had to face up to the implications of sexuality. 'With the adult, as with the adolescent, there can be few emotional complexes in which sex, consciously or unconsciously, open or repressed, explicit or disguised, is not present. And I need hardly say that in the sexual emotion I include that which may exist between man and boy and woman and girl.'

11. 'London Boys at the Colony', Melton Mowbray.

Work in co-educational communities, especially with delinquents, was new. Hoare was more radical than Lane. He saw Lane, often regarded as an anti-establishment figure, as 'representing (and believing in) the capitalist system'. But the two men's similarities were greater than their differences. Both were more concerned with agricultural and domestic training than with academic education. Both worked in a rural setting with calming natural influences. Both believed in love. And - like Baden-Powell's - neither of their experiments survived the War.

4
Ellen and the Law

Bread and dripping for dinner,
Bread and dripping for tea.
My wife says meat and vegetables
Are far too heavy for me.
So one day for my dinner,
She gives me such a treat,
She takes me to the dining-room,
And lets me look at the meat.

East End song

Ellen Stanley was the leader of Lane's new community of hand-picked delinquents. The daughter of costermongers, she came from Deptford. Once, when she was a small child, her parents invested all their money in buying fruit and vegetables to sell at Epsom on Derby Day. Unluckily, Derby Day was a wash-out that year, taking the family's fortunes with it. Soon her parents began spending most of their time out drinking, and Ellen and her younger brother and sister were left to their own devices. Ellen wandered unchecked in the rookeries of Deptford, perfecting her shop-lifting skills amongst the coster barrows and stalls of neighbouring street markets.

Now her fortunes had changed again, and she, Mary and Annie ('the Deptford trio') had to learn to live not only in the country, but with a gang of rowdy and disruptive boys. There seemed to be no help forthcoming from their superintendent, who serenely disregarded any unruly behaviour.

Lane's assistant Mr Jones was less patient. Urged on by the girls one day, he cut a stick from a hedge and went up to the boys' bedrooms. He did not attempt to use his weapon, but indicated that he might do so if further provoked. This had no effect: the noise continued night after night. One evening after 'a particularly trying din', Lane went upstairs to check for damage. The boys feigned sleep. Then one of the sleepers leapt out of bed, shouting "It's all right, boys, it's only Mr Lane". Lane felt sure that he had now been accepted by the boys and that - having gained their confidence - he could begin his work. His function, he said, was 'to encourage all activity, bad as well as good'.

Lane called the first Council meeting ostensibly to consult the citizens about future sleeping arrangements in the cottage presently being completed. Should the boys have a dormitory - since they evidently preferred to share - rather than separate rooms? Surprised at being consulted, rather than told what to do, the citizens began cautiously to give their opinions. Voices grew louder; the discussion ranged more widely. The eldest boy threatened to thump anyone who interrupted him.

At this, the children decided to elect a policeman, rather than a chairman, to run the meeting. Policemen were after all something they knew about. It was then agreed that separate rooms should be retained in the new cottage. There was to be no sharing. One boy requested a private room so that he could hang up his mother's photograph. "If you don't sleep good at night," a girl said, "the next day your face is all crinkled up and you get into rows all day." So noise was discouraged after 10pm.

The children turned to other, more basic matters. It was decided that 'soap should not be thrown about in the bath-rooms or in the passages. Clothes must not be thrown under the beds, but must be hung in their proper places.' The meeting lasted for over two hours. And, as Montagu had promised, the girls voted equally with the boys. So popular were the meetings and so enthusiastically received that at first they were held almost every night. Soon they were divided into two kinds: judicial and legislative.

Ellen became the first judge, a position she held until one of the meetings was referred to as a 'court' and the chairman as a 'magistrate'. At these words, the citizens' sympathies immediately shifted away from the Judge towards the defendant. Lane wrote, 'The witnesses lied valiantly in the interests of the boy defendant and disorder and horseplay broke up the meeting. Afterwards the boys said that no girl had a right to sit in judgement upon a boy, and the girls agreed. The girl judge resigned. What a comment upon the child's attitude towards our adult courts this is!'

12. Ellen Stanley, Judge (right), and Annie Scott, Clerk of Court.

A boy was later elected as judge, but within a few weeks he was deposed, as 'he himself furnished the greater number of cases for his own court and obviously could not judge himself'. Ellen was reinstated. She was a fair and thoughtful judge, who made the punishment fit the crime. For example, several of the girls were accused of leaving a candle burning in a dangerous place. The Judge ordered the culprits to go to bed every night for a week without a light: one of them was Ellen herself.

Her Clerk of Court was Annie Scott, who was only thirteen years old (she had claimed to be fifteen when arrested). She was 'popular, capable, and witty', the quickest of the girls to grasp the communal ideal. When she was fourteen, a gold locket and chain were awarded to her by the citizens in commemoration of her services. Ellen too was much appreciated. In July 1914 the Court Book notes 'Ellen clapped for being a fine judge'. Yet both of these girls had been described by their magistrate Cecil Chapman as being 'thoroughly anarchistic' only one year before.

Most of the London children had been referred to the Little Commonwealth by Chapman, along with Mr Simons at Greenwich and Horace Smith at Westminster. Other children had been referred by W. Clarke Hall, Old Street magistrate and author of *The State and the Child*. The children from Hartlepool had been sent by a magistrate named J.E. Bladon. Some children were referred from Manchester. These Northern children, Lane wrote in 1915, had 'more rugged characteristics' than their Southern counterparts, and could more readily show 'a ready fist and sharp tongue'. All of them could expect to spend two or three years at the Little Commonwealth, unless the superintendent - in consultation with the magistrate - decided to reduce this tariff.

The children were committed for petty offences, like loitering, or pilfering, or wandering. The boys were often gamblers. Some were there because they were neglected, like Cissie Shorter; some were orphans like George Gold from the Scattered Homes in Camberwell and Albert Street, whose father had died at Salonika (his widowed mother died a few months later). Asena Oliver spent her first eight years in the workhouse, whilst Walter Hibbs had spent his entire life there. It was not unknown for the children to be sent to the Little Commonwealth because they had nowhere else to go. Other children had to be sent back to homes that were destitute - a boy called Ginger came from a very poor home to which the authorities were reluctant to return him. Some homes may have been morally dangerous. Lane noted with distaste that Freda Mailer's father sent 'mushy' letters to her. One or two of those sent down to Dorset were innocent. Tom Hammett was referred there even though his case had been dismissed. When no other indictable offence had been committed, a common charge was incorrigibility. In 1914, Lane told the Penal Reform League that 'incorrigibility [was] a label, not a condition'.

13. Cecil Chapman, Southwark magistrate.

The assessments of the citizens' probation officers can sound unreasonably harsh to modern ears. Eliza Butler, sent to the Little Commonwealth for her own protection, is described as 'vain, flirtatious, deceitful'. One of the boys is dismissed as 'erratic, obscene, dishonest and lazy'. Asena Oliver is classified by her former superintendent as a possible 'moral imbecile'. Terms like this used about vulnerable young people make Lane's tolerant, accepting attitude seem all the more remarkable.

The Register of the Children's Court, kept from December 1913 to May 1918, is outwardly a largely unpromising leaf-green ledger, which leaps into life from the very first page. Anyone - child or adult - could make a charge, a complaint or a simple inquiry about anyone else, adult or child. The Judge would then decide what action, if any, to take - and the Judge's decision was final.

There was no jury. Unlike the American Junior Republics, modelled on their country's constitution, the Commonwealth (as its Second Annual Report pointed out) 'adopted a more direct and primitive method of government by the whole group, as is found in the history of village communities'. This method ensured the equal involvement of all the children and avoided the cumbersome formalities of a complex legal structure.

Written laws were drawn up gradually, as required. There were also unwritten rules, such as the one banning boys from the girls' sections of the cottages and vice versa. Rules within the cottage family groups varied from one to another, and were regarded as 'purely household affairs'. There was never a prison, and the policeman's career was short-lived. The system relied on the community's collective disapproval of wrong-doers. Lane believed that prison was 'a place of refuge for the wrong-doer'; the real penalty was facing those you have wronged. 'Each citizen is a peace officer' the Second Annual Report declared, and certainly, a strong sense of community pervades the Court Book. As complaints were not regarded as 'sneaking', bullying, which relies on this negative code for survival, was kept to a minimum. The Judge could punish any citizen for contempt of court. Witnesses could be compelled to make an affirmation: 'I promise in the case before the Court to tell the truth, the whole truth, and nothing but the truth, on my honour as a citizen.' Children normally had to be fourteen to be accepted as a citizen and it was a privilege which could be relinquished or withdrawn. Citizens found to have been lying on oath could be deprived of their citizenship. There was also an appeals procedure.

A special girls' court, excluding boys, could be called at the request of three girls, with a girl judge appointed by the general judge. (The Junior George Republic had a separate girls' court and judge.) A special boys' court could be called in the same way.

Apart from fines, the commonest punishment was to be confined to either Big Bounds, the area of the Little Commonwealth estate, or Close Bounds, the small area bounded by the farmhouse, the school and the workshops. Anyone confined to the latter was not allowed to speak to any other citizen except on business, when a distance of ten feet had to be kept. There was no corporal punishment. When Lane worked in American schools he cheerfully admitted to 'walloping' boys occasionally. By now he had changed his mind.

The register opens on 29 December, 1913 with the Judge herself being warned for throwing snow in the house, a charge brought by Mrs Jones. Tools are left out, apples are stolen and eaten, Charles Goodwin is fined for 'Slovenly dress. Buttons not on clothing' (a charge brought by Lane). Lane also raises several enquiries, such as 'can the Court stop Ted's cheeking guests?' for which the ruling is 'Ted to try to stop'. Questions are deftly put by citizens too. Vera asks, 'Is it right for the boys to catch birds?' (No, it isn't, the Judge decides.) There's a plaintive inquiry from Charles Goodwin addressed to all the girls: 'Who ate pudding for me?' The impression is one of cheerful near-chaos. Children accuse each other of using 'profane language' or 'a very bad word' or of (in the case of girls) 'unladylike behaviour'. 'Rough houses' are dealt with, so are stone throwing sessions and broken windows. But praise is also handed out, mainly by Lane. Donald MacPherson's minutes, he declares, are 'very well-kept'.

The citizens take to their Court with great enthusiasm, and children's natural sense of justice. They seem to have grasped (perhaps through previous experience) the Court's structure and procedures very quickly. Above all, they enjoy having their opinions taken seriously.

Adults are not exempt from charges. Nor are Lane's own children, or Gladys, daughter of Mr and Mrs Jones. Lane is warned for having called Sam Tucker 'a crook'. Mr Jones is found not guilty of leaving the barn 'very untidy'. Scores are settled through the Court, with Sam complaining of Eliza Butler 'swindling me'. Shopkeeper Annie indignantly asks, 'Who said I didn't put my things on my bill?'

A boy on whom the Court was forced to make a special ruling was Ted Dalston. He had refused to work, and his clothes had become torn and dirty. The Court decided that a tax should be imposed on his fellow citizens for his maintenance, with which a new suit of clothes would be bought. Ted grew angry at this judgement, declaring 'I will never wear pauper's clothes', whereupon 'three sturdy boys' removed his rags and dressed him in his new suit. About six weeks later, Ted offered to pay for the clothes. In reaction to the ruling he had taken the responsible job of caring for the horses, and could now afford to look after himself.

Smoking was a recurring problem (Ted was one of the offenders). An early Court ruling was that boys under eighteen and girls under twenty should not be allowed to smoke. This rule was often broken. There was a special court held on 10 November, 1914 after cigarettes were found in Jabez Harriman's room, stolen by him - or Ted Dalston, or Jack Smith - from Mr Pauley, the Commonwealth's carpenter. On 12 February, 1915 Donald MacPherson applied for, and was given, special permission to smoke. (Lane himself was an habitual and heavy smoker.)

In November 1914, a dramatic entry records that Lane has resigned his citizenship, due to differences between 'certain citizens and himself'. He hopes that 'the Commonwealth will go on better without him'. Presumably having made his point, he resumes his full role on 11 December. This gives rise to the question - one which Lane always emphatically refuted - could the Little Commonwealth go on for long without him?

5
Homer Lane

George Montagu's first choice as superintendent had not been Homer Lane, but a man called Harold Large. Contemporary newspaper reports described Large as a social reformer from New Zealand of part-Maori descent, who had until recently been 'one of the chief vital forces in the Stratford-upon-Avon Festival scheme with Mr F.R. Benson, through whom Shakespearean drama and folk-art have once more become a living force in the life of this country'. (Mary Neal, one of the Commonwealth's supporters, was also involved in this movement.) A musician and a footballer, Large was said to be both cultivated and 'yet quite at home' with hooligans. Montagu told Lane's biographer, David Wills, that Large had been discovered by Lord Lytton. Montagu said, 'We didn't like him much' and he went on to describe Large's bizarre habit of adding numbers up in railway carriages 'to deduce omens from them'. Nevertheless, on Montagu's instructions, Large visited the George Junior Republic at Freeville from October 1911 to February 1912. In April 1913 he was reported as being in charge of the Little Commonwealth prior to its opening on 1 June. But then on 28 April, George Montagu told a meeting at the Lyceum Club in London that Large would instead be responsible for the organisation of the school, while Homer Lane with his 'wonderful psychological experience' would undertake the actual training. This might have been a workable arrangement, but unfortunately Large was taken ill, and he resigned on 16 October, leaving Lane in total control.

Homer Terril Lane was born on 22 September,1875 of seventh generation Puritan stock, in Hudson, New Hampshire. He was the second of five children. He spent his boyhood in Framingham, Massachusetts, where his upbringing was strict but happy. He enjoyed

14. The young Homer Lane (wearing spectacles) with his family.

fishing in the fields around the town, and was remembered by his younger brother, Robert, as something of a perfectionist. When planting onions, for example, he would set them in rows exactly two inches apart.

The one great shadow across Lane's childhood was the death of his sister Bessie, at the age of two. One day when he was about eleven years old, Homer and his elder brother Jordan had been left in charge of their little sister in the family garden. Anxious to venture further afield, the two boys sent the child back into the house. They crossed the railway line that bordered the garden to reach the pond which held their newly-built canoe. Their mother, meanwhile, thinking that they were still close by, let Bessie out once more to play. The little girl was crossing the railway line in search of her brothers when she was killed by a passing train. Homer blamed himself; he must never have forgotten the accident.

Yet Homer was a popular and lively schoolboy, and quick to learn. He played the first saxophone ever to be seen in the local band, and had a good singing voice. He was not, however, particularly interested in books. He won a place at High School but left after about a year, to work as delivery boy at Folger's Stores. He had also worked whilst he was a schoolboy: he could turn his hand to many different jobs.

In 1898 he married Cora Barney, second daughter of the Police Chief at Southborough, where he was then living and working as a delivery man and part-time soda jerk at the Center Store. Lane does not seem to have had any other serious relationships as a young man. He and Cora married for love, and produced two children, Raymond, born in 1899, and Cora, born in 1901. Lane also acquired a horse and buggy, luxuries he could ill afford. A year or two later, he bought a family house. Throughout his life he tended to be over-extravagant and careless about his finances. Now even he realised that he needed more money to support his family and blossoming life-style.

15. Homer Lane, grocer's clerk in Southborough.

Encouraged by Southborough doctor, Claude Jones, Lane enrolled at the Sloyd Training School in Boston. His course was primarily practical. Sloyd, a Finnish word meaning 'skill', was a method of handicraft training. Through Sloyd, handicrafts - particularly woodwork - became central to the previously over-academic school curriculum. Sloyd's aims were: 'to instil a taste for and love of labour in general; to inspire respect for [manual] labour; to develop independence and self-reliance; to train in habits of order, exactness, neatness and cleanliness; to train the eye and the sense of form; to accustom to attention, industry, perseverance and patience; to promote the development of the physical powers.' One of the lecturers on the course was John Dewey, who was then teaching at Harvard University, and who became a major influence on the young Lane. Dewey was critical of the existing system of education. It was class-bound and self-interested, whereas it should be an introduction to a life of shared interests and social interaction. The combination of Sloyd and Dewey was central to Lane's developing thought.

This was a happy time in Lane's life until - suddenly, unexpectedly - his wife died of pneumonia following a chill, caught riding in the buggy. Although grieving, Lane was not to be diverted from his new-found career. After a short period as summer relief teacher of woodwork at Pennsylvania State Reformatory, he started a part-time Sloyd School in Southborough. He had not been impressed by the reform school system, which seemed to him only to make bad boys worse.

As a Sloyd teacher, Lane moved from Southborough to a school a thousand miles away, in Detroit, Michigan. Around this time he got married again: to his first wife's elder sister, Mabel. It has always been assumed that this marriage was for practical reasons - Mabel was obviously not his first choice - but she remained loyal to the end of his life. Two more children were born: Priscilla (Polly) in 1904 and Allan in 1907. Lane spent 'a considerable time' during this period in the babies' ward of a hospital, 'making a special study of the problems of nursing and weaning and of infants' activities'.

In 1905 he was briefly appointed as Superintendent of Playgrounds in Detroit. His observation of the children there led him to conclude that 'by far the greater proportion of juvenile crimes are merely a form of play'. In their unsupervised games, the children's heroes were 'the bandit, the pirate, the outlaw and the robber'. Lane was dismayed to discover that delinquency declined in cities with unsupervised grounds. His investigation of this discovery led to an interest in the ideas of Maria Montessori with her theories of the relationship between work and play.

16. Homer Lane, superintendent of Public Playgrounds in Detroit.

A pro-abortion remark, made probably in the heat of the moment, resulted in pressure being put on Lane to resign. It was suggested that the subject was of more than theoretical interest to him. Despite the lack of any evidence, Lane resigned without protest. However, he soon found work with the Solvey Guild, which had been set up primarily for the welfare of the employees of the Solvey Process Company.

Moving on yet again - restless yet purposeful - Lane became a woodwork teacher at the Hannah Schloss settlement. He experimented with some early forms of self-government in the clubs he began for the boys of the settlement, which was in a tough, Jewish neighbourhood of Detroit. In a piecemeal way he was acquiring knowledge of new educational ideas, with emphasis on the practical, the social and the democratic.

Through Schloss, he became involved with the Boys' Home and d'Arcampbell Association (motto: 'A Fence at the Top of a Precipice is Better than an Ambulance at the Bottom'). In a move apparently initiated by Lane, the association was transferred to an old country farmhouse twenty miles from Detroit. Lane drew up plans for a new building, which he constructed with the boys' help, mixing concrete and making breeze blocks. This became known as Ford Hall, and the institution as the 'Ford Republic' after its benefactors who were a wealthy family (unconnected to the motor trade. The place later

17. Homer Lane at the Ford Republic.

changed its name to the Boys' Republic to avoid any confusion about its patrons.) Lane became superintendent, while Mabel acted as matron.

At the Ford Republic, self-government was gradually introduced, though of a more rigid kind than that afterwards applied at the Little Commonwealth. It followed the lines of the American constitution, in the system pioneered by the more famous George Junior Republic. Lane later denied that he had known anything of the latter place, and may indeed have shaped Ford out of his own developing philosophy. As in the Little Commonwealth, control was economic, and the school and its finances were often chaotic.

Lane was in his element. But then, once again, disaster struck. Lane was forced to admit to an affair with Miss Bingham, a fellow teacher who also acted as his personal secretary and with whom he had 'an intellectual affinity' he had not found with his second wife. Once again, Lane made no attempt to save himself or his career. He left the Ford Republic and went to work, punishingly, as a navvy in Buffalo, leaving his wife to continue as the Republic's matron. He supported Miss Bingham, who was pregnant, until the baby was born. Lane never forgot her, or their child. In Buffalo, he seems to have re-thought his life.

The American part of his career was over. Having visited the Ford Republic, George Montagu invited Lane to England to talk about his work - and to act as consultant to the Little Commonwealth, which was then just beginning to take shape.

6
Building

The Little Commonwealth began with high hopes, with confidence and ambition. The outward and most visible sign of this was the building plans.

In the very early days, the children were housed in the original farmhouse - renamed Bramble - to which an extension had been added. New cottages were built to the west. They were originally thatched, until October 1915 when a fire broke out in Bracken one afternoon. The men and boys were out working in the fields and raced back when they heard the news. They stood on neighbouring roofs to stamp out any sparks and saved most of the furniture. Thereafter the buildings were roofed with slate.

Directed by Lane, the boys worked on making roads across the estate, on a courtyard at the back of Bramble, and on the drains. One of the girls worked briefly at carting flint, but then gave up and returned to household duties. Despite the promises of the prospectus, boys and girls stuck to their traditional roles during the first years of the Commonwealth.

Water was obtained from springs in the chalk hills, with a temporary supply from a catch-basin in the spinney to the front of the farmhouse. 'We have erected an engine and a pump there, and laid a temporary main to a tank in the house with a capacity of 600 gallons. The pumping-engine is of three-horse-power, driven by petrol.' This was the machine in the charge of 'Engineer' Harry Billen. Later there were plans to install a larger engine of six or eight horse-power and to make a reservoir with a capacity of 15,000 gallons. This would have supplied not only the Commonwealth, but also the village of Batcombe. The community had its own postbox, and was literally on the map.

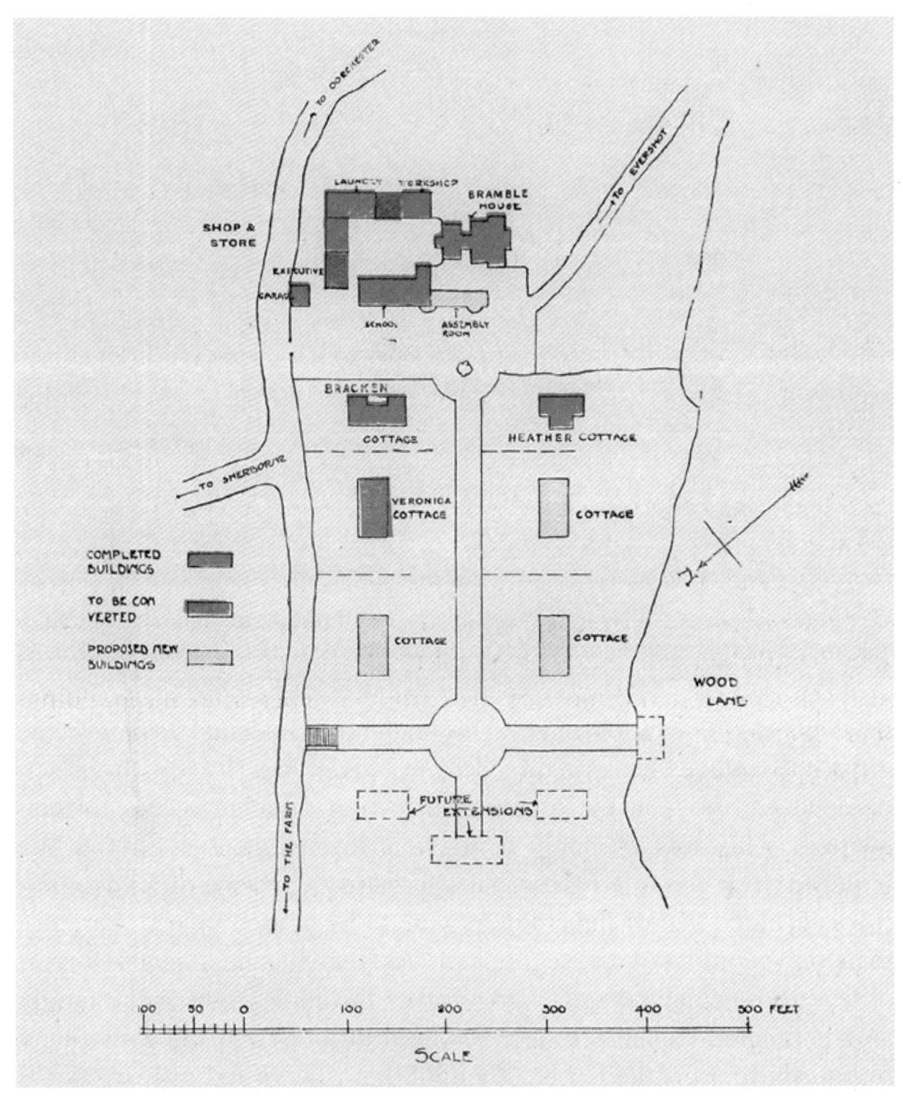

18. Plan of the Little Commonwealth.
The light grey buildings were never erected.

Eight cottages were planned - three were built - around a market square. The architect was Charles Henry Biddulph-Pinchard, who specialised in domestic buildings, and who continued his involvement with the Little Commonwealth by serving on the aftercare committee. The first cottage to be completed was Bracken, under the patronage of

19. General view of the Little Commonwealth. Heather Cottage, left, and Bracken centre - behind Flowers Farm, which was renamed Bramble. The long building to the right was the carpenter's shop and steam laundry.

the Duchess of Marlborough. This had been intended to house the girls, but cottages became mixed from November 1913, with girls at one end and boys at the other, each having separate access to their quarters. This was probably a practical arrangement at first, while building work was in progress, but afterwards it became official policy. It was decided that, if the children were to be housed in 'real' families, then they could not be segregated. As the Second Annual Report observed: 'The natural self-expression of the adolescents in the family are sublimated by the presence of the little ones and the consequent responsibilities entailed.' Lane thought that if boys and girls lived and worked together, then they would take each other for granted. The 'romance and mystery of sex' would be muted. The Report claimed that the Commonwealth was the first place where such comprehensive co-education had been tried in a 'corrective community'.

Solidly and attractively built, with Arts and Crafts trappings, the cottages were also impressively well-equipped, with furnishings chosen mainly by Alberta Montagu. An inventory of 1915 - 1916 for

Bramble cottage lists complete sets of cutlery, salt cellars, sugar tongs and fish kettles. Breakages are also listed: dinner services were constantly being broken - deliberately or otherwise - and having to be replaced. Godwin's China Shop in Dorchester is a recurrent creditor in the accounts.

The sale catalogue drawn up at the Commonwealth's closure includes such items as Windsor chairs, oak book shelves, a bamboo cabinet with folding doors, six chromolithographs and two oleographs, a library of books including the forty-eight volumes of Scott's *Waverley Novels*, a cottage pianoforte by Bord of Paris, and a number of feather pillows and quilts.

Since most of the children came from desperately poor homes, they had almost certainly never encountered soup spoons or cruets before. When Homer Lane went to visit Ellen's parents in Deptford, he had to drink his tea out of the teapot lid, as the family's two tea cups were 'too badly cracked to be offered to a guest'.

20. Bracken Cottage before the fire.

21. Making the courtyard.

After they had first arrived, children tended to be clumsy and forgetful, with very short attention spans. A staff member in the later years, Elsie Bazeley, who had been a tutor at Whitelands College in Roehampton, noted their 'lack of discrimination in the purpose of things - a pillow-case would be used for a table-centre, an electric light shade for a flower-vase, a window-curtain for a blower for the fire, a table-knife to chop wood'. Even some of the other citizens objected to such behaviour. An entry in the Court Book accuses Bertha Cohen of 'using basin and tea cloth to scrub office'. It was noticeable that as they became happier, and better adjusted, so the citizens learned to use tools and household equipment more effectively - though china continued to be broken until the end. And sometimes the cottages would become wildly disorganised and grubby. When this happened, visitors must have doubted the efficacity of the Commonwealth. Nothing was usually done until the inhabitants of the offending house were threatened with unemployment. Then would come the cleaning. Miss

Bazeley has described how much the citizens loved clearing-up, which they did with great vigour and zest.

'Every available inch would be scrubbed and scrubbbed hard; everything possible would be polished - windows, tables, cupboards, stove. They knew exactly where all the dirty corners would be, and had them all out relentlessly. They went beyond the demands of utility and took an aesthetic pleasure in their doings; even the cocoa-tins would be polished...' Lane believed that this untidiness was only to be expected - the disorder of the place where the children lived reflected the disorder of their minds. Dealing with one would help the other.

A 'motor house' was built for Lane's Ford car, which had been given him by a supporter. Like Lane, his car must have had a local celebrity, as he sped around the countryside: motoring 'hell for leather' was one of his few means of recreation.

Workshops were also completed early on, and the steam laundry, of which Ellen was sometime manageress. Citizens who did not wish (did not know how to?) do their own washing, could pay to have it done 'at the usual rate per piece'. This was a very necessary service, as bed-wetting and faecal incontinence were common amongst the children, particularly at the beginning of their stay.

Another important building was the shop. The shopkeeper, boy or girl, would be one of the most intelligent and sensible of the citizens. For most of her stay at the Commonwealth it was Annie Scott. Yet, as Elsie Bazeley noted, even such a citizen 'invariably arranged the packages in the shop as a child of five would have done; that is, blue, orange and red packets were arranged to make the prettiest patterns on the shelves, without any reference to their contents'. Both shop and fittings were donated and installed by Lane's fellow-countryman, H. Gordon Selfridge. Selfridge came from a Middle West background not dissimilar to Lane's New England one; Selfridge's biographer described it as a place where 'For young and old, work was the clarion call, a brassy imperative summons from Jehovah echoing across the wide spaces. Idleness was sin and damnation. Work was consecrated endeavour.' An enthusiastic supporter, Selfridge also paid for the shop's coinage, which was an aluminium version of the real thing. He then backed a 1915 scheme to grow lavender, according to the Second Annual Report. This does not seem to have flourished, as it is nowhere mentioned again.

Through hard work - and a flair and showmanship also not unlike Lane's - Selfridge became a wealthy man. In 1909 he opened his great emporium at the Marble Arch end of Oxford Street. This was the first purpose-built department store in London, with twenty-one window displays, lifts, a roof garden, an ice cream soda fountain, a perfumery and a reading room. Another innovation was the staff council, where any problems could be discussed, with representatives from each of the store's 130 departments. Selfridge may have come to hear of the Little Commonwealth from a member of his staff. The chief receptionist Percy Nash had been stage manager for the actor Herbert Beerbohm Tree, who had performed in a fund-raising matinee for the Little

22. Dinner-time. Showing the interior of Bramble Cottage.

23. Children gardening outside the shop.

Commonwealth in the early days. Or he may have heard of it from his advisor, Herbert Morgan, who was in charge of the advertising department of W.H.Smith: C.H. St John Hornby, a partner in Smith's, was also a subscriber to the Little Commonwealth.

There was no church or chapel, though the citizens were expected to attend religious services. As superintendent, Lane would have been obliged to arrange for church attendances for the citizens. The practice, too, would no doubt have been encouraged by deeply-religious members of the Committee, like Lord Lytton.

In February 1914 four Roman Catholics, including Ellen, were taken by car on Sundays to the church of the Sacred Heart in Sherborne. Envious of this privilege, some of the other children were keen to convert to Catholicism. Non-Conformists walked to Hermitage where there were two mission-rooms: one Wesleyan and the other Non-Denominational. (One still survives: a sturdy brick building, used as a store.) Other children, the great majority, went to Batcombe church.

On alternate Sundays, the vicar of Batcombe and Frome Vauchurch, the Revd Joseph Pulliblank, came to take services at the Little Commonwealth. According to the Court Book there was a lot of bad behaviour - giggling and horseplay - at these meetings. In Alice Woods' *Advance in Co-education*, Lane wrote: 'In the beginning church attendance was general. Later but few were regular. Then at a suggestion of the vicar a law was passed compelling attendance. This law was finally rescinded. Religious services were then held in the community itself, which during some periods were well, and during others poorly, attended. Sometimes family prayers in the cottages were a part of the daily routine...'

For most of the children, religion was just one of the many methods of control which had been applied to them in their short lives. Ellen was a devout Catholic, Lizzie Marden and one or two others were confirmed whilst at the Commonwealth, but they were in the minority. For Lane, the failure of the children to show any signs of spiritual growth was a cause of bitter regret. He had hoped that they would move naturally from a world of social values into a spiritual one. It was perhaps too much to expect of them. Miss Bazeley said that they had 'not a shred of private life' and a hatred of solitude. They lacked inner resources: they had previously had no opportunity to develop them, and for most of them, by the time they reached the Little Commonwealth it was likely to be too late.

Lane's personal attitude to religion is less clear. Of Puritan descent, and brought up in a devout household, he had joined the Congregational Church at about the age of fourteen, a move probably encouraged by his mother. But later he turned against formal religion. Miss Bazeley thought 'The whole of life was to him a religious experience, and religious observances were left behind as schooling had been. But he felt that they were a natural medium of growth and orientation for youngsters, and whenever he could he tried to make them think about these things, but without success.'

Certainly the doctrine of love was as central to Lane's philosophy as it would be to to that of any more orthodox practising Christian. Lord

Lytton wrote that he believed Lane to be 'the most complete and fearless exponent of Christian love as a principle of conduct and rule of life'. Towards the end of his life, Lane had begun writing a book about his philosophy of life. This was never finished, but in 1934 Lord Lytton incorporated the existing fragments into his own book *New Treasure*. He argued that Lane 'had no literary gifts' and that the passages which remained were 'too unorthodox to be intelligible without further elaboration', which he then went on to supply. He wrote that although Lane lacked 'the spiritual force that men call religion', he was conscious of this lack, feeling that the Little Commonwealth would be 'incomplete' without a spiritual dimension, which Lane himself could not provide. Lane had an abhorrence of the doctrine of original sin - believing as he did in original goodness - and had no faith in the 'supernatural character of Christ'. Nor did he believe in eternal life with its uncertain promise, consigning the majority to hell, and thus casting a shadow over many earthly lives. His faith, as his life's work showed, was in the innate goodness of human beings.

Lane too often saw the damage wrought by orthodox religion on children in his care. He told J.H. Simpson in a letter of 1916 that whilst Freud blamed sex for psychological disturbances, he himself felt that 'religious torment' was equally responsible. He thought that Christianity was too bound up with morality; for which Lane substituted love. Christ had been crucified because he, too, had made this substitution. Lane's love is not 'the love of the poets or romance' but an attitude of mind, one which Lane himself had been fully able to develop.

(Lane comes very close sometimes in his last years to identifying himself with Christ.)

7
Recreations

How, then, did the citizens fill their spare time? Lane did not believe in organised leisure: after their day's work the citizens spent the evenings as they chose.

One frequent activity was absconding - particularly in springtime. Both Lane and Montagu accepted this as natural, despite the bad publicity it created. They believed that the truants were mainly running away from themselves and their problems. On 27 November, 1913, a few months after the Little Commonwealth had opened, the *Dorset County Chronicle* reported that at Cerne Abbas petty sessions, before Lord Digby, Wilfred Charles Goodwin had been accused of stealing a bicycle belonging to Arthur Augustus Warren, a plumber who was working at the Commonwealth. Goodwin later tried to sell the bicycle in Yeovil. In his defence, the local physician, Dr Dalton, told the court that the boy 'was in a serious state and could not hold his own with the other boys'. Goodwin, who was described as 'hopelessly incorrigible' and who had been transferred from Nottingham Gaol, where he was being held for theft, went on to abscond several more times. He was released into Lane's custody: the usual outcome for the truants.

Time after time Lane and his colleagues would patiently collect the wanderers from Yeovil or Sherborne or Shepton Mallet, even from as far away as London. When they returned, truants were usually placed on Close Bounds by way of punishment, and taxes would be levied on citizens and staff to cover the cost of collecting them. There were regular columns in the Commonwealth's account books for 'Damage', 'Truancy' and 'Police Expenses'. Lane's policy was not to make a fuss about this.

The Little Commonwealth should have been a difficult place from which to escape. Truants seemed instinctively to head northwards, to push away from the heavy-browed ridge above the Commonwealth or the neglected easterly woods around Minterne, choked with hazel and sycamore: the setting for Thomas Hardy's *The Woodlanders*. The whole area around Batcombe, Hilfield and Hermitage has looked towards Sherborne and Yeovil as its market towns, ever since the early enclosure of their common lands when new and wider lanes were built. The pull is in that northward direction.

Southwards, up on the edge of the ridge sits the Cross in Hand, a small silent emblem, carved in Purbeck marble. Its purpose is unknown, though there are endless theories about it. Perhaps it is the remnant of an old cross, its upper limb lost - an old preaching cross, the stone replacement for an earlier wooden cross, which had served as the church of the district before parish churches were built. Or it could mark the site of an ancient burial ground for the same reason (from the stone, the tower of Yetminster church can be seen). Thomas Hardy's first wife Emma, fond of theories, believed it to be a plague stone.

24. The Cross in Hand, Batcombe Down.

The Cross is commemorated in Hardy's poem, 'The Lost Pyx', which retells the local medieval legend of a priest who went out in stormy weather to give the last sacrament to a dying man. On his journey over Batcombe Down the priest loses the pyx (container of communion bread) but on reversing his footsteps finds it again, lit by 'a clear straight ray' and surrounded by worshipping beasts. So afterwards in an act of thanks 'He reared this stone to mark where shone/ That midnight miracle.' The priest is from Cerne Abbas, a place which, with its ruined monastic church and its lewd giant, mingles Christian and pagan in a peculiarly Dorset hybrid, both dark and comic. Hardy himself, despite his previous poetic treatment of the subject, blithely points out in a letter to the editor of *Somerset and Dorset Notes & Queries* that 'some antiquaries have from its shape conjectured its origin to be phallic, and not Christian at all'.

The Cross in Hand has also been suggested as the site where 'a criminal was hung in chains for highway robbery and murder committed there'. Still remote even today, in the 19th century the road was described, as 'a wild unfrequented place, much affected by the smuggling fraternity, the furze which grew around forming a good covert for the concealment of the brandy kegs'.

Around here, the sacred can barely restrain the profane. Batcombe church has its own share of supernatural legends, concerning 'Conjurer' John Minterne, the village squire. Minterne made a pact with the Devil and, with Satanic help, leapt on horseback from Batcombe Down over the church, breaking one of the tower's four pinnacles as he jumped. The pinnacle subsequently proved unnaturally difficult to replace. When Minterne died, he was buried half inside the church and half outside it, precisely as he had demanded.

Such uneasy legends, and the weather which can sweep suddenly along the ridge - the mist and the rain - made this a forbidding exit. So the truants found their way northwards through the enclosed, dreamy southern reaches of the Blackmore Vale, stretching into the blue distance. They went along the wide drove roads and the little winding lanes which go nowhere in particular. In spring - truancy time - the verges are rich with wild violets and garlic. There are springs and streams everywhere, reedbeds to trap the unwary, and marshy copses of withies. Hazels and alders grow profusely (the latter were used for clogs and cigar-boxes), the soil is loamy, the landscape never-brown and always watery. Around nearby Chetnole and Leigh in winter, as Barbara Kerr evocatively put it, 'oozing ponds and over-flowing streams seem to set the whole area afloat: moorhens take possession of the fields as jackdaws claim a ruin'.

25. Batcombe Church below Batcombe Down.

It was a difficult, thinly signposted terrain for city-bred children, but somehow they managed to make their escapes. Other citizens made shorter journeys. There are records in the Court Book of visits to the New Inn - down a Batcombe track - for lemonade and biscuits, or, more adventurously, to the Good Hope Inn at Hilfield for 'liquors and cigarettes'. The landlord of the Good Hope in the wartime years was Charles Child. In 1965, his daughter, Mrs Ivy Cornick, recalled those far-off days: 'My father had to go out to work to help us to live, he thatched hayricks and broke in horses. Some of the years at the Inn were very exciting with Irish and Portuguese evacuees who were working in a cover at Hermitage, cutting pit props. They used to visit the Inn each evening.' In the wartime years, the Good Hope must have been an unexpectedly cosmopolitan place.

For those who did stay in during the evenings, there were gatherings in the family houses, or in the assembly hall. Children would get together in the sitting-rooms of their houses, to read or play the gramophone or cut out pictures. Miss Bazeley described the scene: 'we were just a circle of friends gathered round the same lamp and fire. Mr Lane used to sit at his desk writing, or in his armchair reading or thinking and, of course smoking, whilst the citizens were engaged in various distracting pursuits about the room': this was perhaps the first family some of the children had known. The *Daily Mail* of 26 December, 1913 reported on the community's first Christmas, when the tree was 'ruthlessly stripped of all its fruit' by excited children, and there was 'dancing in the courtyard' and a dinner of 'roast pork and

26. Schoolroom, used mainly as an assembly hall.

apple sauce, roast turkey, sprouts, potatoes, plum pudding - and sweets'. There were further celebrations for Lane's thirty-eighth birthday, when 'all the cooks in the Commonwealth' made him a cake with slippery white icing, a bowl of potted salmon and 'huge bread sandwiches with slices of cold raw onion inside'. These refreshments were served after a 'great singing party'.

In the following summer of 1914, 'some twelve of the more reliable citizens' camped out in the grounds in tents supplied by Gamages at a cost of £36. This was 'to facilitate building operations'. Camping is the only outdoor recreational activity mentioned. There is no reference to any sport being played. In 1919 Lane said that the citizens showed no interest in it, yet in his lectures of the period, he stresses the importance of sport. And sport is habitually regarded as a useful outlet for adolescent energies.

During the early years of the Commonwealth, there had not been much emphasis on education. Most of the citizens were older than the usual school leaving age of fourteen, but most of their education had been lamentable - of the learning-by-rote, ruling-by-rod variety, which was current in National Schools of the period. A rural Scottish school of this type is described by A.S. Neill in his *A Dominie's Log* of 1915. 'Tonight after my bairns had gone away, I sat down on a desk and thought. What does it all mean? What am I trying to do? These boys are going out to the fields to plough; these girls are going to farms as servants. If I live long enough the new generation will be bringing notes of the plese-excuss-james-as-I-was-washing type....and the parents who will write them went out at that door five minutes ago. I can teach them to read, and they will read serials in the drivelling weeklies; I can teach them to write, and they will write pathetic notes to me by and bye; I can teach them to count, and they will never count more than the miserable sum they receive as a weekly wage. The "Three R's" spell futility.'

Commonwealth children were often academically backward, and in need of remedial teaching. Lane claimed that they were not bookish and hated arithmetic. In fact he was biding his time until they began to request education for themselves. And eventually - as Lane had hoped

- the citizens did pass a law making attendance at evening classes compulsory. After the initial enthusiasm, lessons began to pall. The citizens still felt that there should be a school, and compulsion to attend it: they could not envisage anyone going willingly to school. Eventually, it was agreed that every citizen should learn some subject, but that they could do so in their own cottages. Subjects chosen were mostly practical: dress-making, shoe-mending, business correspondence. Lane himself gave talks on 'the upbringing of little children'. He also entertained the citizens around his fireside in Bramble with tales of his own youth. He told of how he had run away to live with the Ojibway Indians, or with lumberjacks in Maine, or on a sugar plantation in the West Indies. His daughter Cora said that he had intended to sail to England in 1912 on the Titanic, but changed his mind at the last moment. They were gripping stories and the citizens loved them - even if none of them was true.

8
Casualties of Peace and War

In his public talks, given over the Little Commonwealth years to educationalists and those interested in penal reform, Lane gave varying accounts of the behaviour of individual citizens, accounts which relied on the spirit rather than the letter, telling the story in the manner he felt best suited his audience. This was particularly noticeable in the case of sixteen year old Jabez Harriman, a boy fighter from West Hartlepool, where he had been known as 'Kid Slugger'. Jabez was admired amongst the other boys for his 'heavy and skilful fist'. He was daring, bad-tempered and inclined to be a bully. Though an enthusiastic labourer, he refused to attempt any work which required training. Lane, who was temporarily acting as his housemother, decided to challenge him. Lane said that he had been forced to confront Jabez because he was a boy who needed 'more special treatment than the citizens were able to apply'. There are four different versions of the way in which Lane handled the situation, from the very simple - as summarised by David Wills - to the short story. Wills described how '[Jabez] took from another boy a watch he was taking to be mended, and more or less deliberately smashed it. Lane, seeing this, said something to the effect that if he was so fond of breaking watches he could break Lane's. This the boy refused to do in spite of pressure, and this event was a turning point in his career.'

27. Two young men in the carpenter's shop (now a chapel).
Jabez Harriman is on the right.

Lane told a more elaborate version of the story to one of Lord Lytton's sisters, Lady Betty Balfour. It involved the smashing of china as well as of the watch. A fuller version still was related by Lane in a talk given in South Kensington in 1916, which was modified again in another talk in 1919 or 1920. In this final version, Jabez's friends intervened to stop the cottage china being smashed, and blamed Lane for creating the situation. When Lane countered by producing his own gold watch, Jabez refused to smash it. 'His unconscious and irrational desire to smash authority by smashing property was now dissolved.' Thus, Lane wrote, 'the real nature of boyhood gentleness', of which Jabez was ashamed, had triumphed over 'his old ideal of braggart boastfulness imposed upon him by unsympathetic surroundings'. The real Jabez possessed a 'lovable gentleness with little children, and an affection for animals'. The stories reveal as much about Lane as about Jabez Harriman. Lane had a remarkable empathy with tough young boys, whom he could help by identifying with them.

After this crucial encounter, Jabez became a carpenter, a good one, and was Judge of the Citizen's Court when he left the Commonwealth as soon as he was old enough to enlist in the Army. He became a private in the 2nd Rifles Battalion and his letters home to his friends were those of 'a decent, good boy'. He died at the Front in May, 1916. By 1915, nine of the older boys - and the estate's farmer - had enlisted in the Army and three in the Navy. One boy, Will Sharp, signed up for twelve years. Mr Jones also enlisted in 1915, but returned to the Commonwealth before the War's end. The farmer, Thomas Booker, died of pyrexia on board a hospital ship in the Dardanelles in October, 1915. Percy Machell, a member of the General Committee, died in France.Young men from the Commonwealth killed in the Great War were Robert Brewer, an orphan who developed pneumonia after enlisting and came back to the Commonwealth to recuperate; Charles Goodwin, who continued to write and visit after enlisting; and Donald MacPherson. (Robert Brewer, ironically, had been described by Lane as 'always thoughtful of his skin and careful to keep out of any trouble'.) Donald, from East Dulwich, had been sent to the Little Commonwealth for three years for theft. He was a capable young man, who thrived in his new environment. After two years he was taken on as the member of staff in charge of the mechanical department, and in this capacity could have avoided the fighting. An entry in the Committee minutes of 30 May, 1916 notes that 'Donald MacPherson had refused to allow Mr Lane to ask for his exemption and was therefore going to war'. He joined the 3rd Dorsets, was wounded in June 1917, and killed in the following October. A memorial in Batcombe Church commemorates all five of these deaths. And there must have been more, unsung, fatalities: many other boys enlisted after they had left the Commonwealth and were never heard of again.

A further death occurred inside the Little Commonwealth. George Swift, described by George Montagu as a 'bright, jolly, promising boy', died of blood-poisoning on 30 November, 1915, after being ill for a week. Montagu described how he 'got a slight scratch to his knee', which then swelled up. He developed a high temperature and a fever, recovered briefly, and then relapsed when 'Cerebral symptoms set in which ended fatally'. During his last days, Mr and Mrs Lane watched him in turn, until a nurse from Dorchester took over his care. Montagu paid tribute to the boy, who he said was nicknamed 'Roffy' and was universally popular, being regarded as something of a humorist. He was buried in the Catholic graveyard in Sherborne. The Little Commonwealth paid for his funeral, which cost £9/2s/6d.

George Swift was attended by the Little Commonwealth's doctor, Dr E.E. Dalton of Cerne Abbas, Medical Officer and Public Vaccinator for the area. Remembered as being tall, mild-mannered and a keen cricketer, Dalton had given up the usual pony and trap for a single-cylinder De-Dion motor car, which was driven around his large practice by his chaffeur, Fred Vine. Dalton's was one of the first cars to be seen in the district. His abandoned stable became his dispensary, 'cobwebs and all'.

Dalton was paid £20 a year for administering to the citizens. Surviving medical records, filed by him for the Home Office referrals in 1917, are somewhat perfunctory. One boy is said to be deaf and underdeveloped. Nearly all the children have been vaccinated and they show no signs of physical abuse. These 1917 children had been in the care of institutions for some time; it is likely that earlier Commonwealth admissions showed signs of more serious medical problems. Henry Chapell, for instance, was ill for several months in 1915-16. (For Cissie Shorter's medical diagnosis, see Appendix II.)

This was not a period in which public health was improving. Conscripts during the First World War were frequently found to be undernourished and in as poor a state of health as private soldiers of the Boer War.

9
Suffer the Little Children

Amongst the mainly adolescent citizens of the Commonwealth was a group of much younger children, some of them still babies. These were the Montessori children, whose presence in the community seems to have been a rather impromptu arrangement.

The Montessori movement was new. Its founder, Dr Maria Montessori, was the first woman to qualify as a doctor of medicine in Italy. She revolutionised the concept of pre-school education with the establishment of her *case dei bambini* (Children's Houses) in the slums of Rome in 1907. By 1914, there were Montessori schools in Milan and Verona, as well as eight schools in Rome. The children in her classrooms were provided with miniature furniture, scaled down to their own height, along with miniature household equipment, which allowed them to explore the adult world on their own terms. Given this sort of environment, Montessori believed, the children would prefer work to play. The teacher's role was to observe and guide this exploration, rather than direct its course. This would encourage children to learn for the love of learning, rather than for the love - or fear - of the teacher.

Along with bespoke domestic furnishings, the Montessori system required whole sets of apparatus for academic learning - number rods, geometric shapes, musical bells and sandpaper letters. Children were allowed to learn at their own speed, individually rather than in a group, working their way through the materials.

Montessori's ideas spread rapidly outside Italy. The original English Montessori school was established in August 1912 at the Old Hall, East Runton, Norfolk. Less than a year later, the Montessori Society proposed that the Little Commonwealth should incorporate one of its schools, and this proposal was accepted. Bertram Hawker, who became an active member of the Executive Committee of the Little Commonwealth, was founder of the English Montessori Society, and it was his drawing-room at East Runton which became the first school. The Society sent Miss Tasker, a Montessori teacher who had received 'a year's special instruction' in Rome, to gain practical experience in Dorset. The Little Commonwealth's modest experiment in the new method was thus one of the earliest in England.

The Montessori children were originally expected to remain at the Commonwealth for a year from late 1913 to 1914. In fact, the scheme lasted almost as long as the Commonwealth itself.

Where did the childen come from? Contemporary newspapers claimed that they were 'motherless and fatherless'. They were 'nine babies rescued from disreputable homes'. In the Second Annual Report they are described as being 'collected from the usual sources requiring institutional care', but in fact not all the children were abandoned or orphans. The expenses of 'little Jack Layton' were partly paid by his grandmother Mary, who lived in Bromsgrove and corresponded regularly about him. As with the citizens, some of the Montessori children's relations were simply trying to do the best they could for their children within their limited means.

The children are often referred to - in the Court Book, for example - as 'the babies', and in some cases this was literally true. Olive McLaughlin was sent to the Little Commonwealth at the age of eleven months. She was the daughter of a young mother who had been housemaid to Mrs Margesson (a Commonwealth supporter), and of a soldier who had been killed in France.

Another Montessori child was Tommy Barkess, whose mother, Eleanor, then living in Stoke Newington, was asked to pay a contribution towards his upkeep in August 1917, as he had grown out of the Montessori stage, when children were 'helpful to the girl citizens'. His mother offered to pay five shillings a week, explaining that she could not afford more as she had another child to support - a crippled girl. She withdrew Tommy shortly afterwards and asked for a rebate.

Tommy had become too big to be 'helpful to girl citizens'. Bringing out the maternal instincts of the girls was regarded as being one of the main functions of the Montessori children. The new cottage, Bracken, opened on 6 December, 1913 for nine children, by which time the schoolroom with its stage, distinctive round chimney and verandah was also nearly complete. The Montessori children were taught in a schoolroom in Bracken, and were housed amongst the citizens. The families in each cottage were made more complete by the introduction of small children - and the results proved beneficial. The Second Annual Report notes that 'one girl citizen formerly of an indifferent and unsympathetic nature has been completely transformed through caring for the children'.

28. Mabel Lane outside Heather Cottage with Montessori children.

The children were later housed together in Heather Cottage under the care of Mabel Lane, where they continued to be well-provided for. Amongst the expenses listed in 1915 are 'Babies' clothing £1/7s/1d and Montessori furniture £1/13s/0d'. By December 1917, only three children were left.

It is likely that Lane had no say in the establishment of the school, as the decision was taken at about the time he was appointed superintendent. Lane, as David Wills has pointed out, could not have found the 'relatively cold, academic personality' of Montessoriappealing. And as someone who relied on his instincts, he could hardly have been in sympathy with the system's somewhat rigid methods. In a guarded reference to the method in his lecture on 'The Age of Loyalty', Lane suggests, characteristically, that the system might work if the teacher used it unsystematically.

Certainly, Lane's ardent disciple, A.S. Neill, greatly disliked the 'didactic apparatus' essential to the system. In 1926, he wrote to Bertrand Russell whose *On Education* had just been published:

'I do not share your enthusiasm for Montessori. I cannot agree with a system set up by a strong churchwoman with a strict moral aim. Her orderliness to me is a counterblast against original sin. Besides I see no virtue in orderliness at all. My workshop is always in a mess but my handwork isn't. My pupils have no interest in orderliness until they come to puberty or thereabouts. You may find that at the age of five your children will have no use for Montessori apparatus. Why not use the apparatus to make a train with?'

Neill enjoyed being outrageous; Lane was obliged to be more sympathetic. Like Montessori (and Neill) he placed great value on the importance of acquiring manual skills. But the Montessori method was alien to him. Montessori teachers would - unobtrusively - pre-arrange their groups of children and shape any problems in ways that minimised disruption. Lane on the other hand proscribed as little as possible. Yet the two methods, different as they were, worked side by side at the Little Commonwealth, and both were to have far-reaching effects on education.

10
Some Visitors

The Commonwealth and its Montessori School attracted many interested visitors. When the experiments began, overnight guests had to stay at the Acorn Inn in Evershot, but soon paying guests were housed in Veronica Cottage. Guests were also housed in Heather, the smallest of the cottages.

The first and last visitors to the Commonwealth were both priests. The American ambassador Walter Page visited early on, as did the magistrate Cecil Chapman and his wife, Adeline. Newspaper reports are scanty after the opening year, but it seems that earlier visitors were predominantly those rich and fashionable people interested in good causes who had helped to fund the Commonwealth. There were many of them, in spite of the difficulties in reaching a place so remote. The citizens were the subject of much attention, particularly in the first twelve months of the Commonwealth's life. This in itself attracted notice. Writing in *Pall Mall* in March 1914, Filson Young, who was a supporter of the scheme, warned of the dangers should it become too fashionable. The children 'simply must not be studied by the public, as a hive of bees or a colony of ants is watched through a glass panel'. The result of such intense scrutiny would be that the citizens would come to regard themselves as 'interesting and important sociological specimens'. This did not seem to happen, but they must certainly have enjoyed the sustained attention, which could have done wonders for their self-worth.

Later, it was the professional workers with children who came, many of them inspired by Lane's lectures. Two of these were the teachers A.S. Neill and J.H. Simpson. A.S. Neill often told of how he spent a weekend at the Little Commonwealth in the winter of 1917, while he was a cadet at the artillery school at Trowbridge in Wiltshire. The visit changed his life. 'I sat up until four in the morning listening to him.' Neill said that from Lane he learnt of the necessity of being on the side of the child, although his books, from *A Dominie's Log* onwards, show that he had already taken that attitude himself. Neill also said that Lane taught him to 'get at the motive of the child'. An experienced teacher, Neill was turning in the direction of delinquent children, and he planned to work with Lane at the Commonwealth once the War was over. Perhaps it is fortunate that this never happened: Neill was to say that he could not begin his real life's work until after Lane's death.

29. A.S.Neill as a young man.

Lane had a great effect, too, on J.H. Simpson, a teacher at Rugby School, who first heard Lane talk about the Little Commonwealth 'to an audience of 200 public school boys' at Gresham's School, Holt, in September 1913. Lane spoke 'with hands in trouser pockets, the broad shoulders slightly bent forward, deliberately and with something of a drawl'. Simpson 'rather diffidently' asked at tea if he might visit. He first went to the Commonwealth after Christmas in 1913 and continued to go there often, even buying the citizens a motor bike. His observations are especially valuable because, although he admired Lane and his methods, Simpson did not fall as completely under his spell as other observers were wont to do. Simpson noted that Lane was so impartial that he himself made several visits before he realised which were Lane's own children. Lane was devoted to the children. 'If he met a child', Simpson told David Wills, 'his face would light up'. Simpson thought that the community was at its best in the opening stages, and that later on Lane was 'grossly overworked'. He also thought that Lane's methods sometimes cost troubled children too dearly.

30. Approach from the Batcombe side,
with Homer and Mabel Lane and Mr & Mrs Jones.

Inspired, Simpson began to experiment with self-government at Rugby School. He was able to do this because his headmaster, Dr David, was another of Lane's admirers. He was also encouraged by Norman MacMunn, a further visitor to the Commonwealth (who was to work after the War with traumatised orphans at Tiptree Hall in Essex.) Simpson's experiences were recorded in his books *An Adventure in Education*, 1917, and *School-master's Harvest*, 1954. The boys concerned were aged between thirteen and sixteen. Though normally well-behaved and hard-working, they seemed to Simpson to be 'mentally unalert, and to be almost pathetically submissive to conventions'. Like Neill's 'bairns', they were being shaped for a pre-ordained way of life.

Simpson used the form as his basic unit, as MacMunn had suggested in his *A Path to Freedom in the School*. This brought its own problems - especially for an establishment like Rugby where the house was the dominant unit. He wrote, 'although our new approach made it far easier to make some of the lessons cooperative rather than competitive, the "work" as a whole could hardly seem to the boys a matter of common interest'. So his form were then given charge of 'orderliness, punctuality and efficiency', but this was still not enough.

Lane, with whom Simpson was corresponding about the experiment, advised him that his scheme would not work unless 'the errors of the individual' brought 'a penalty to the whole community'. He suggested that a level of academic achievement should be set for every boy in every subject. Collective success would be rewarded with form holidays. Simpson, who was not an enthusiast for conventional marking systems, responded enthusiastically. The idea worked; Simpson regarded the experiment as a success, and felt that he had learned from his experiences: 'I had learnt, first of all, some of the obstacles to be overcome by anyone trying to introduce 'self-government' inside the public school world. On the other hand, I had learnt how much it could do, even when applied in a small way, to weaken unnecessary and absurd conventions, to bring out the shy and hesitant, and to modify what is rather misleadingly called schoolboy conservatism.'

If the Rugby experiment was something of interesting oddity, Simpson was to take it much further at Rendcomb College. This Gloucestershire school was founded by Noel Wills as a boarding school for rural elementary school boys of the county. They would be given 'certain advantages and opportunities which are commonly enjoyed only by the sons of wealthy parents'. The boys received their full board and clothing free of charge. They were soon to be joined by fee-paying boys from preparatory schools - and this social mix proved of benefit to both parties.

31. The experiment attracted much attention in the early years.
1. Preparing ground for the plough. 2.The 'Policeman'. 3. Making new roads.

Simpson described his experiences in *Sane Schooling* (1936). He saw that any experiment was coloured by the personality of its leader, since education in practice is an art rather than a science. Only Lane could have made the Little Commonwealth work; his system of self-government suited his personality. Simpson was dealing with ordinary boys, who had different educational needs. He had to find the right method to suit them and himself. He had thought that it might be difficult to establish self-government without the economic discipline of the Commonwealth, and without the overhanging fear of a known 'worse alternative', but found that his boys responded quickly, grasping the benefits of the scheme.

Self-government at Rendcomb centred on a General Meeting at which all the older boys were present. Simpson was there in the background, but seldom interfered. The judicial body was the Council, which had only seven members. Simpson had attended Court sessions at the Commonwealth, where he thought that there had been occasions when a private talk with a child might have worked better than the 'public agonising' of the meetings, which could serve only to make matters worse.

Neither did Simpson give his boys the option of not attending lessons. They were being prepared for life and its obligations. If they did not continue with their lessons, he told them that they would merely be wasting the work of their earlier years - and most of them would need to gain a school certificate. In such ways, he shaped for himself and his boys a self-governing system suited to their mutual needs.

11
The Trouble with Girls

As well as those killed in the Great War, at least nine other young men from the Little Commonwealth had enlisted in the Army or Navy. In this way at least, the community was a microcosm of the world outside, as some of its brightest and best were lost. Left behind were the younger or feebler boys, boys like Edwin Down, described by Miss Bazeley as 'small, pale, weak' (and missing his mother). The Third Annual Report of 1916 remarks on the imbalance, noting that now the older boys had left, their replacements were younger or 'of an inferior calibre'.

But boys continued to hold the more technical and responsible positions of Engineer and Public Works Officer. Boys worked on the farm - with cows and dairy, pigs, calves and sheep, horses and carting, ploughing, sowing, harvesting, hedging and ditching, tree-felling and hauling, building and carpentry. The girls' duties were restricted to the houses, the shop, the laundry and, eventually, the garden.

One of the gardeners was Miriam Waller, usually known as Minnie. Miss Bazeley describes her as 'a big, rather hulking lass' from Hartlepool, with a 'heavy, rather lowering expression'. She had been committed to the Commonwealth by her father and stepmother, after 'she began spreading totally false stories' about her stepmother's relationships with men. On her arrival she caused great trouble to Ellen, her housemother. Then she was set to gardening work where, despite persistent quarrels with the garden foreman, Cissie Shorter, she was suddenly at peace.

During the harvest, Homer Lane employed Minnie to help him, because she was bigger and stronger than any of the remaining boys. Miss Bazeley noted: 'That silent, exacting, finished work in the field was extraordinarily good for [Minnie]; impulsive strength was compelled to integrate itself to keep pace with the almost relentless drive of machinery, carrying out an intelligent purpose. One cannot idle with machinery; if one is careless the result is immediately manifested.' Hard physical labour suited Minnie. She would box and wrestle with the boys, and was as strong as any of them. Her later position as a housemother was not so successful because it gave her 'too little scope for her energy and too much opportunity for clashing with other people'.

32. Girls' sewing class.

Of the original Deptford trio, Ellen Stanley and Mary Derbyshire both became members of staff after their sentences were completed. So did Lizzie Marden. Lizzie, who came from West Hartlepool, had been charged with theft. Left in charge of the house during her mother's continual absences she had become 'wilful beyond control and dishonest'. Yet all three of these young women were to become excellent housemothers. Mary was praised as 'warmly sympathetic and kind'. Miss Bazeley likened Lizzie to Wendy in *Peter Pan*, a serious figure, unselfishly fussing over the young boys in her household. Sometimes she became totally wearied by her role. In June 1917 Miss Bazeley wrote: 'This fatigue is a factor in the community life perhaps not enough allowed for, unless one realises how isolated and forced in upon themselves these town children are by being suddenly plunged into country life. Very few of them really identify themselves with the country spirit; though they have been set in a place of wide horizons they scarcely become adopted into a larger life, they bring with them the short-sightedness of the slum and the self-absorption of those who have always lived in a crowd. This fatigue cripples the advance of the community life, and the chief cause of it is the smallness of the community'.

It might have been different if the community had grown larger, as Montagu had planned and the War had prevented. As it was, the citizens seldom developed individual private lives; theirs remained the life of the street: public, volatile and gossipy, as Miss Bazeley noted. '...The smallness of numbers and consequent poverty of ideas encourages these children's already abnormal taste for the most outrageous gossip and increases their inclination for violent quarrels and their tendency to import personal antipathies as a motive into the conduct of public and private life.'

33. To the left, Annie Scott in the shop.

Among those who adapted most readily to country life were Ellen Stanley and those of the boys who were keen farmers. Another person who became intensely involved in this new life was Ethel Moore, once described by Lane as 'the sharpest thorn in the bush'. Ethel was sent to the Commonwealth in 1914. She had committed no crime, but was sent there for her own protection, having been removed from 'dangerous surroundings'. Her mother was ordered to hand over all her children, and a younger sister, Jean, was afterwards sent to the Commonwealth. Ethel was technically discharged on April 1st, 1916, but stayed on as a citizen helper - first as shopkeeper and laundry manageress, and then from August 1917 in the office. Ethel gradually took over the accounts along with the rest of the office work and her small neat handwriting can still be seen in many of the ledgers. Like some fictional postmistress, '[Ethel] had access to everything, knew everything, opened letters...' All of the graduate girls - but particularly Ethel - enjoyed pivotal positions within the community and became forces to be reckoned with.

Other less able girls were liable to move from one job to another, and from one cottage to another within the Commonwealth, as they were allowed to do if the other cottage residents agreed. In the short term, and especially in cases of personality clashes, this system worked well, but once the girls left the Commonwealth it could cause problems with their employers.

Commendably, members of the Committee did not abandon former residents, but tried to keep an eye on them. A Commonwealth Club for ex-citizens was established in George Montagu's London home at 8 Portman Square where a woman called Miss Carter worked indefatigably to help them. In 1915, Montagu wrote to Lane about Annie Scott, who had by then left the Commonwealth, but who seemed unable to settle down.

'I feel there is a tendency in our girls who have gone to show a rather spoilt attitude in meeting the world...I think the whole subject wants talking over, whether the independent spirit which the Commonwealth seems to foster does not tend to make it more difficult for them to meet life outside...This may be a more marked characteristic of the girls than the boys. It may be that the time is too short to get steadiness - whether we are right to allow them to change their work so often at the Commonwealth and get taken on at other jobs too readily is another question that wants thought, I think.'

In the space of two years, Annie worked in a bottle factory, which she found 'too rough', then at a butcher's (he turned out to be an alcoholic) and briefly in a leather factory. She then went to Mrs Leggett's as a kitchen maid for '£16 a year and two dresses', but left unceremoniously, because she was worried about her younger brothers and sisters at home with their inebriate father. (Another ex-citizen, Eliza Butler, more successfully took her place.) Throughout this period Alberta Montagu continued to help Annie, who next became seriously ill with scarlet fever. When she recovered she found a job in a skin factory for 17/- a week. Then she became engaged to a soldier and was last heard of working at Woolwich Arsenal.

Miss and Mrs Margesson, two other patrons of the Little Commonwealth, had a similar experience to Mrs Leggett. They wrote that the girl citizen they had taken on as domestic help had not received any systematic training in cleanliness or cooking. She was 'quite willing in a sense, but didn't know any better'.

The very first citizen of the Commonwealth, Vera Cooke, also proved difficult to place, if for different reasons. Montagu wrote to tell Lane that Vera had left Gamages department store. This was not the first job she had abandoned, and Alberta Montagu tried to find her factory work instead. Vera was staying with her sister-in-law - her brother had enlisted - and she needed to find work. Montagu feared for her and wrote, 'I am dreadfully sorry about Vera - when I saw her she struck me as if she were going downhill. She had a haggard, callous look on her face, as if she were chucking up the sponge.'

Vera, who had been classified as mentally deficient, should not have been sent to the Little Commonwealth at all. At some point in her unhappy tale, she was charged with collecting for charity and disappearing with the takings, for which she was sent to prison for two months. She was later sent to the Elizabeth Fry Home in Highgate, after which no more is heard of her.

Vera's was a special case. Annie Scott and girls like her were restless because life at the Little Commonwealth, where they were treated as individuals, well-housed and well-fed, left them with expectations which they were unlikely to realise in the outside world. Domestic work within a community family was very different from lowly skivvying in a London household. This dislocation perhaps affected girls more than boys because there was such a narrow range of jobs on offer to working-class women, all of them laborious and ill-paid. The boys at least had a wider choice. As the War went on, more openings became available to women, in transport, offices and munitions, but girls still tended to be sent into old-fashioned domestic service - probably because they could be placed in the homes of ladies sympathetic to the Commonwealth. Mrs Margesson, for example, was a member of the General Committee; Mrs Leggett had helped to fund a cottage. Several girls became nursemaids - Lane and his Committee retained their faith in girls' maternal instincts. Ellen Stanley and Mary Derbyshire loved their jobs with children at Lady Isabel Margesson's; other girls were less enthusiastic, or totally unsuited to such a role.

Elsie Bazeley thought that the Commonwealth's Committee expected too much too soon from the citizens. It took a very long time to heal most of them - longer than their period of detention. They might be returned to society before they were ready.

In addition, educational opportunities at the Little Commonwealth were very limited, the emphasis being placed on acquiring practical skills. The children were tested on admission by the Binet-Simon system, which, in a series of thirty tests, assessed them according to their mental, rather than their physical age. This should have shown which children might benefit from further academic education. Despite his high school education and his own obvious intelligence, Lane did not rate formal learning very highly. Children such as Jane Bird were nearly illiterate, but Lane made no effort to remedy the situation, mere noting 'we are not well equipped for formal education of a scholarly kind'

Lizzie Marden was the only citizen given any further education during the day. She went for a while in 1915-16 to the Convent of the Sacred Heart in Sherborne, along with Lane's two daughters, and then to Weymouth High School. Lizzie was described by her social worker as backward 'due to home life'. When her mother wrote to her asking for money, Lizzie wanted to leave school and go to evening classes instead, so that she could earn money to send home.

More intelligent children were usually selected for the Commonwealth, as it was thought that they would take full advantage of the self-governing system. Annie Scott had shown early promise. Along with her friends Ellen and Mary, intelligence was one of the qualities for which she had been selected. And there was at least one other girl who might have benefited from more education - if only to occupy her mind. That girl was Bella Griffin.

12
Bella Griffin

The moon shines bright on Charlie Chaplin,
His boots are cracklin',
For the want of blackin',
And his little baggy trousers they want mendin'
Before we send him
To the Dardanelles.

First World War song

Bella (Rosabella) Griffin was committed to the Little Commonwealth by her parents in June 1916, when she was sixteen years old. She had gone beyond their control, staying out at night and engaging in 'general disorder' on the streets of Walworth. A leather-stitcher in Aldgate, Bella was charged with stealing a pair of boots from her sister and was sent to the Commonwealth for two years. Her parents contributed to her upkeep. Bella was 'tall, graceful, shrewd, and rather cruel' according to Miss Bazeley. The citizens nicknamed her 'Charlie' because of her ability to imitate Charlie Chaplin to perfection.

Bella could mime well, and dance, and sing the sharp or sentimental songs of the East End music halls. All of these talents made her popular with those citizens who preferred socialising to studying in the evenings. Unruly, irresponsible and combative - like many a girl of her age - she became the natural leader of any opposition to the status quo. Bella first clashed with Homer Lane one night when she draped herself in ghostly white garments and woke up two of the younger girls. They were so terrified that they had become hysterical: at which point Lane was forced to intervene. Bella had, Miss Bazeley wrote, 'a quite impossible sense of humour'. Lane did not see the joke. He was not amused by either Chaplin or his namesake. Yet Chaplin, like Bella, came from Walworth, and had spent most of his childhood in extreme poverty, some of it in the grim surroundings of Lambeth Workhouse (a place he had managed to escape without resorting to crime). Lane seemed not to notice the pathos behind the slap-stick in the adventures of 'Charlot,' Chaplin's tramp.

Bella was probably bored, and was certainly ill-equipped for country living. She had been removed from Walworth's bad influences, but she remained better suited to East End life - if not East End music hall, on the boards of which she might have been a clever performer. To find herself in damp and misty countryside, scantily peopled, without cinemas or shops, must have been dismaying and unstimulating for her.

34. Lambeth Workhouse. Some of the citizens had known life in surroundings as grim as these.

To occupy Bella, Lane decided to give her a position of responsibility. She was made housemother at Veronica in June 1917. He explained later: 'I wanted [Bella] to have every opportunity for developing her influence to that point in which its results would be apparent to those under her influence. A suppression of her influence would have merely postponed the breaking out of the tendencies that were apparent at the time.' His plan was only partially successful. Bella was at first a model housemother with very high standards, standards impossible for her to maintain permanently; keeping a spotless cottage with gleaming stove and floors. Miss Bazeley praised her tenacity and also her pugnacity: 'a very necessary quality for a house-mother'. But 'her trouble-making tendencies soon brought her family to grief', and they appealed to Lane to remove her from her position. When he made no response, the household staged a hunger strike. Bella went on to garden work, and to ferment more trouble. Lane had underestimated her spirit.

Whenever trouble flared, Bella was there, taking the side of the disaffected citizen. She was manipulative, and a natural street-brawler. Miss Bazeley, tolerant and affectionate as she usually was to some very troubled or difficult citizens, clearly found her very difficult to like. But Lane, as usual, continued to see the good in her. 'Underneath all this rough exterior, however, was a very nice nature. She was generous to a fault, extremely loyal to her particular friends, and always sympathetic with those who were in trouble with the government.' As it turned out, this was a more than generous tribute. In his darkest moments, he would describe her very differently.

13
The Home Office

On 26 January, 1917, Lane received a letter from the Reformatory and Industrial Schools department of the Home Office:

'Dear Mr Homer Lane,
I am writing at once to say how thoroughly [we] enjoyed our visit to the Little Commonwealth and for myself, how much I benefited from our lengthy conversation.
While I do not see eye to eye with you in every respect (I do not suppose I ever shall do) I am immensely impressed by the great value of the work you are doing and in particular by the appearance and manners of the children, for it is evident to me that something has been driven out and something else put in: in other words, that your methods have the effect of driving out the evil and implanting the good, and I have much pleasure in recommending the Secretary of State to agree to the Little Commonwealth being certified as a Reformatory for 45 children...
Charles E.B. Russell.'

Charles Russell was no rubber-stamped bureaucrat. He had worked as leader of boys' clubs in Manchester from 1892, and written sketches about his 'Manchester Boys' which had later appeared in book form. He had been a member of a Departmental Committee on Reformatory and Industrial Schools. This practical experience, and his own independent mind, made him a highly unusual Chief Inspector, a post he had held since 1913.

Even so, Russell's letter came as rather unexpected news to the Commonwealth. The Home Office was not usually sympathetic to fresh ideas, especially ones so conspicuously involving the presence of adolescent boys and girls and girls in close proximity and the absence of conventional discipline. Lane's persuasive words in the 'lengthy conversation' referred to by Russell had once again worked their magic. It was gratifying for the Little Commonwealth to be recognised for the value of its work - and then there was the prospect of extra money.

Contributions to the Commonwealth had been dwindling because of the War, as they did to all ventures not concerned with the war effort. This problem had been partly countered by a 'godparents' scheme. A godparent would pay towards the upkeep of a child and in return was supposed to receive regular information about how the child was faring. But still money was hard to find.

The possible advent of 45 more children also meant that the Little Commonwealth might have achieved its originally planned quota of about a hundred children, though in fact it never reached its target. Only 94 adolescents were admitted over the five years of the Commonwealth's existence, and some of these stayed only briefly, as they were found to be mentally deficient or otherwise unsuitable.

From June 1917 the Commonwealth received 19 Home Office referrals, a number of whom had been in and out of Borstal and other institutions and were possibly beyond help. These 'especially difficult cases' formed half of all admissions and an effect of this was to upset the Little Commonwealth's balance. Many of the earlier citizens had been referred by sympathetic magistrates, who had assessed them for their suitability. For these most recent, more random incomers, it was perhaps their last chance.

Lane, as usual, saw this as a welcome challenge. On 1 April, 1918, he wrote to Lord Sandwich (as Montagu now was) about the recent influx. 'The Home Office have been sending us especially difficult cases that have been discarded from their other reformatories, thereby indicating that they have more than the usual confidence in our school.' They were, Sandwich later agreed, children with whom 'other institutions had successively failed to cope'. Like Lane, Sandwich regarded them as being different in the depth of their problems, rather than in the type.

Of Laura Green, sent from Ipswich Girls' Reformatory, Homer Lane wrote to the Home Office on 30 October, 1917, that she was not of the right mental calibre for the Little Commonwealth and would have to be treated 'quite separately'. She was incontinent, and absconded almost daily 'sometimes only partly clothed'. She never went far when she ran away, being found at nearby places like Frampton, Maiden Newton or Sherborne, as if hoping to be traced. And yet despite the evident depth of Laura's distress, Lane did succeed in helping her. By the following March, he said that her psychological disorder 'was almost cured' and that she had become 'amiable and docile'.

Another Home Office referral was Asena Oliver, transferred from Coventry Industrial School for Girls in 1917. She was thought to be 'particularly difficult', as although she was only fourteen, she had spent six years in various institutions. Before that, she had been a workhouse child. No one knew the whereabouts of her parents. She was described as 'half gypsy, half tramp', but despite her forlorn history was 'small and healthy, strong and bright'. She was fond of reading - and her exploits would have made a book.

One day Asena had entered a house in Leamington Spa and hidden herself under the dining-room table, where she had stayed while the unwitting occupants were eating their evening meal. Once they had gone to bed, she stole objects from all over the house, then went into the kitchen, cooked an egg for her supper and packed herself a parcel of food. After stealing some clothes, she put them on, leaving her own behind her. She also cut 'a valuable plush coat down to her own size'. (This kind of behaviour was remarked upon by Cyril Burt in his book *The Young Delinquent*, 1925. 'Many delinquents suffer not from too much, but from too little fear. They are reckless, headstrong, and venturesome.' Due to lack of intelligence, or of imagination, the child is 'literally fool-hardy'.)

Asena's cheeky thieving, which continued at the Commonwealth, was said to be intermittent. Stealing, as J.H.Simpson observed, occurs at times in every school and has very little to do with whether the child comes from a rich or poor background. 'It is almost invariably a symptom of something deeper.' In Asena's case it was obviously caused by a lack of love, but was also disruptive to the community. Otherwise her behaviour was good - although she did tend to abscond very frequently. The problem of girls absconding as well as boys was one which came with the Home Office children. But when the final trouble came, it was not these children who were the catalyst, but some of those - those girls - who had been there for the longest time.

The Little Commonwealth was inevitably changing. So were Lane's plans for it - insofar as they were ever formulated. Originally he saw the Little Commonwealth not as a place for long-term stay but more like the Ford Republic had been. In January 1914 he wrote in the *Penal Reform Quarterly Review* that he hoped citizens would not remain for the full term of their sentence (given here as three years). 'In the Commonwealth were undoubtedly ideal conditions, and if they stayed there so long that they became dependent upon this for their happiness, and the Commonwealth did not fit them for their future place in life it would do them more harm than good.' By 1917, though, the Little Commonwealth had become, in Miss Bazeley's words, like a 'frontier farm': all energies were concentrated on it. Lane's aim by now was self-sufficiency, both materially and socially.

As the wartime shortages took effect, the farm became increasingly important. The land was described in 1917 as being 'all pasture except for Whiteway Bottom - arable - Withy Bed - wood'. In the same year, for insurance purposes, eleven cows were listed - all Shorthorns or Devons with names that included 'Little Cow, Kicker, Newman, Strawberry, Rose, Honey, Crumpet, Daisy, Cherry, and Cressy'.

The garden was increasingly important too, though its produce could never be wholly relied on, as Miss Bazeley described. 'The very large and productive garden was in the charge of the head garden girl and was entirely worked by girls. The field out of which it had been formed had originally been ploughed and fenced by the boys, but from that point the girls took it over and worked it very successfully. The garden provided a large part of our food; the amount of meat imported into the Commonwealth was reduced to a minimum during the last eighteen months and we lived very largely on vegetables. We also counted on the garden for a certain amount of money income. Our onion crops were quite valuable in the later war period. But, as in other Commonwealth ventures, no counting definitely on one's harvest was possible; a day or two's carelessness, and the most hopeful prospects might be destroyed.'

Sometimes accidents happened in the most well-meaning manner. Cissie Shorter, garden foreman, read in a new garden magazine about how to eradicate pests from French beans. However, instead of spraying her beans with an emulsion of paraffin as directed, she (not understanding the word 'emulsion') took a bucket of paraffin from the shop and poured it, undiluted, over the crop. The result was, as Lane described it, 'a scum of lovely petroleum colours on the surface of the ground, the beans having entirely disappeared'.

Undeterred by such homely disasters, by gates being left open and by forgotten tools rusting in the rain, Lane farmed on, almost single-handedly. He had strong support from his farm foremen, latterly Russell Blunt, but many of the younger boys proved work-shy.

Lane was much influenced by the ideas of Heinrich Pestalozzi (1746-1827), who stressed the importance of social development, and believed the life and work of a school should be like that of a family. Perhaps also because of his personal experiences, Lane had hoped and expected that 'some of the best of the older boys and girls, as they became young men and women, would marry, build cottages and form families, and that these fresh young families would be the most valuable of all the forces in the life of the Commonwealth village.' The Commonwealth buildings had deliberately been laid out in a village pattern and Lane, after all, had brought his own wife and four children there. Raymond, his elder son, had gone to Sherborne School, but returned during the holidays and worked there when he left. The others were brought up at the Little Commonwealth - and Lane's younger son Allan wanted to be a farmer. One flaw in this vision was that Lane did not seem to take seriously enough the existing relationships, however damaged, between the children and their parents, or their probable homesickness, or their concern for their brothers and sisters.

But in any case the War put an end to hopes of new families settling there. By 1917, as the Little Commonwealth's balance became tilted, this ideal - despite the flourishing of some of the children - had become unattainable. Apart from Miss Bazeley, who had taken a cut in salary when she moved to the Little Commonwealth, and who was perhaps more than a little in love with him, Lane was not well served by his staff in his efforts to achieve this end. Mr and Mrs Jones, for instance, were at times actively hostile to his plans.

The atmosphere had begun to change during the previous year, as Lane had been aware. In the early days, the Court was more effective and the community, with occasional unobtrusive intervention by Lane, was self-policing. Now the Court and other meetings had deteriorated, due to the small number of citizens taking part. And though the rules of the two main punishments, 'Big Bounds' and 'Close Bounds' had already been revised in March 1915 at two special legislative sessions, the Close Bounds rule never really worked. It cut across the ethos of the Commonwealth by isolating an individual and diminishing him or her in the community's view. Fines were probably a more effective deterrent, but, like Close Bounds, they could punish the debtor's families, as they were ultimately responsible for payment.

Lane was also concerned about how the citizens would be employed after dwindling funds brought building work to a premature end. He undertook several measures to improve morale. In April 1916, he proposed to Montagu that they introduce a student teacher community into the Commonwealth, to spread his ideas and to fill the educational void. Then on 26 May, 1916 and again on 27 October, 1916, Lane took the extreme step of imposing 'Reformatory Rules' on the Little Commonwealth. This meant running the Commonwealth strictly according to Home Office rules, with the children being treated as inmates rather than citizens and with the Superintendent in absolute charge, dealing directly with all complaints himself. The intention was to show the children just how preferable the Commonwealth regime was to any official one - and for a while, it worked. But not for long: a general malaise had set in.

14
Relationships

Lane had never worked with girls before. He had shown that he was undoubtedly capable of handling the roughest boys, often by joining their gang, and thereby 'spoiling the fun'. He could be as tough as they were, and they respected him for it. But girls were a different matter.

Lane of course had two daughters, Cora and Polly. Polly, the younger of the two, was often at the Little Commonwealth when not at school, though how much time Lane spent with her is a matter of conjecture. He was 'Daddy' to so many of the children that he may not have spent much time alone with his own offspring. And ironically, the fact that they were housed in family units meant that the Commonwealth's only conventional family did not all live together: Homer and Mabel Lane were in charge of different cottages.

During their stay at the Commonwealth, some of the girls grew into young women and, naturally enough, they began to pair off with boys. Lane had been confident that daily proximity would discourage such behaviour, and this might have been the case if the girls and boys had been together since infancy. As it was, they first met in their early teens. During the day, they were more or less segregated due to the male/female division of labour. But it was different in the evenings.

As citizens could decide for themselves how they spent their leisure hours, some of them opted to spend their evenings studying or reading in their own houses. But the majority went to the assembly hall. Beth Jones was in charge of this group. Her husband entertained the children with comic readings, which proved very popular. Lane disapproved of the readings, just as he disliked Charlie Chaplin: he was serious-minded. According to Bertram Hawker he had a marked sense of humour, but it was of a quiet, dry, kind.

The assembly hall gatherings became rowdier, without the restraining influence of the more studious element. Citizens danced and played games. During the dancing they began to pair off. Lane listed the offending couples, their names like lovers' carved on a tree:

Ellen and Robert Brewer
Ethel and Bill Potts
Bella and George Gold
Minnie and Alfred Carr

Such predictable adolescent behaviour seems to have come as an unpleasant surprise to Lane, perhaps because it was so unlike his own youthful conduct. To discourage these habitual pairings, lessons in Morris and folk-dancing were organised, and these proved popular for a while. The lessons were led by a teacher who had been sent to the Commonwealth by Mary Neal.

35. Mary Neal.

Mary Neal was the founder - with Emmeline Pethick, another Little Commonwealth supporter - of the Espérance Girls' Club, which taught drama and dancing to London working girls. The two women had also set up a tailoring business called 'Maison Espérance', employing girls in unusually fair working conditions. After Pethick married Fred Lawrence, Herbert MacIlwaine became Neal's assistant. He was responsible for the notation of the dance movements in *The Morris Book* (1907) which he co-authored with Cecil Sharp. MacIlwaine copied the notations from one of the Espérance girls, whose teachers had been Morris dancers themselves. Mary Neal believed in going back to original sources. She was for some years a vital force in folk dance revival, which became highly fashionable.

The citizens therefore had some excellent teaching. But as an American, Lane obviously knew very little about Morris dancing, with its cuckoo's nests and cuckolds, nutting maids and ladies of pleasure. The dancing might have used up some of the citizens' energy, but it would scarcely have taken their minds off sex. When the attractions of these activities palled, the citizens returned to their previous pairings. Bella was a leading spirit in this move.

Then Lane noticed that they were also 'playing kindergarten games such as "Drop the handkerchief", "Jolly Miller" and "Winking" for hours at a time'. This should not have surprised him; babyish behaviour was a common reaction to sudden freedom. Cyril Burt, who visited Hoare's community at Riverside, remarked in *The Young Delinquent* that 'No spectacle could be more pathetic than a party of full-grown boys and girls, of sixteen years and over, plunging into babyish buffonery more appropriate to a child of six, hiding and seeking in the attics and the cellars, parading about with paper helmets and wooden swords, digging smugglers' caves in the garden...' They had not been able to play in their young childhoods, having nowhere to go. Only two per cent of Deptford, for instance, was open space.

Lane did realise that it would be a mistake to close the assembly hall in the evenings, but he continued to disapprove - and to make his disapproval plain. Beth Jones, who thought Lane a kill-joy for encouraging study in the evenings, resigned twice during 1916 and 1917 over the issue. She had clashed with Lane before; theirs was obviously a difficult relationship. Lane also had arguments with her husband. But he stuck to his opposition to couples getting closer: 'I felt that it might become dangerous in that it would destroy the usual delicacy of sex relationship among adolescents upon which we depend for the regulation of relationship between the boys and girls of the Commonwealth.'

It proved a mistake to disparage individual relationships in this way, and turned those involved against him. How intimate they became is unknown. Some of the girls were there because of their behaviour on the streets, and Lane himself thought that Minnie had already had intercourse with a soldier before she came to the Commonwealth. Cissie Shorter alleged that Minnie would 'do anything' with Alfred Carr, but then Minnie and Cissie were notorious for their bickering. Minnie said that she felt sorry for Alfred, and was irritated by Lane's interference. (There is, incidentally, no record of any pregnancy in the Little Commonwealth.)

Quarrels were very prevalent in 1916-1917, and Bella maximised them. She succeeded in driving a wedge between Lane, Ellen and Mary, so effectively that the two girls left the Commonwealth. Bella and three of her friends refused to garden under Cissie, giving as a reason the bad language that she used. They particularly objected because they said she was swearing in front of Ethel Moore's sister Jean, a child of ten. They involved the child in their story, and this angered Lane. The girls were put out of work.

Petty enough; but this incident was to have far-reaching results. Bella then persuaded one of her cronies, Iris McIntosh, to write to her mother, saying that she had been 'insulted' by Lane, and that she was in 'great danger'. Iris had been sent to the Commonwealth because of her 'kleptomania'. She had a violent temper and her arrival in 1917 had presented the community with a new problem: 'a fighting girl'. Bella also wrote to her own parents, saying that Lane was an 'improper' person and that her friend Iris's mother would corroborate this charge. Her aim was to persuade her parents to remove her from the Little Commonwealth.

Iris's mother duly arrived, and proceeded to behave in a high-handed and hysterical manner. She took her daughter, with Bella and another girl, Bertha Cohen, for walks during working hours and deliberately ignored a Court meeting. She declared that she was taking her daughter home as she was 'overworked'. As she was entitled to do so, Lane could not prevent her.

36. 'Merrie England Once More'.
Punch cartoon by Bernard Partridge, 13 Nov. 1907.

Bella also drew in Ethel Moore, one of the girls angry with Lane for teasing her about her relationship with Bill Potts. Touchy, serious, Ethel did not like being criticised. Having Ethel on her side was quite a coup for Bella as Ethel was an important and well-respected citizen.

Lane, who usually worked by instinct and theorised later, here seemed to be applying a plan of action without due regard for those involved, and he failed to ease the situation. Could he have been jealous of the girls' growing relationships? Since the departure of so many older boys, he was very much the dominant male, a man in his prime, and a warm and attractive figure. Many of the girls were in love with him at one time or another. Now they were looking elsewhere.

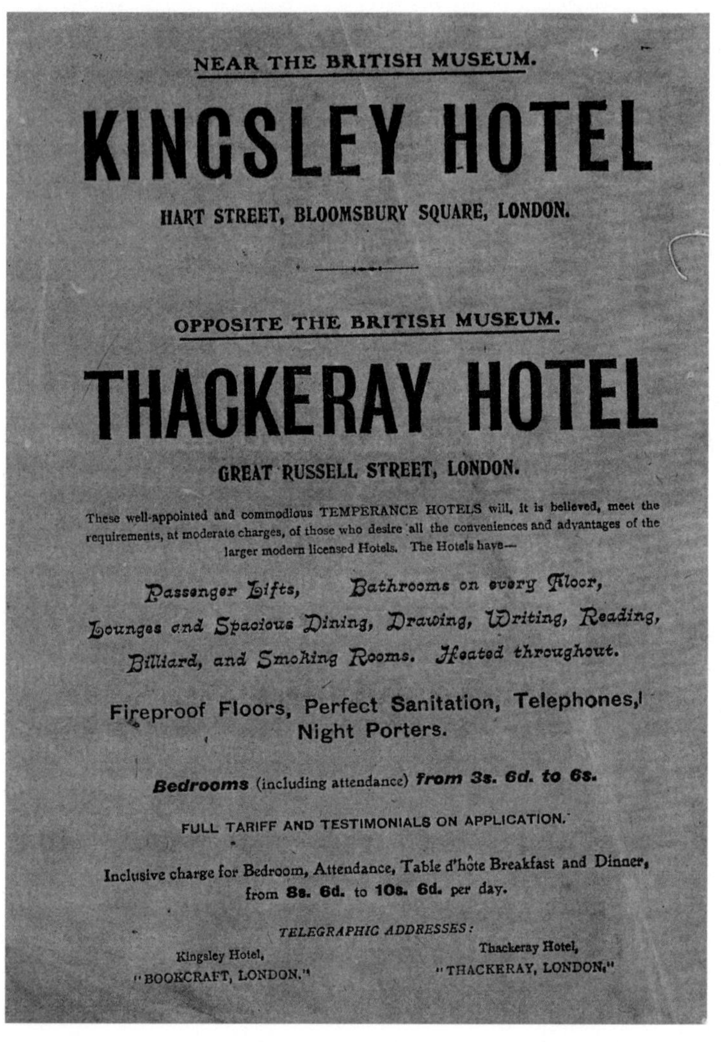

37. Advertisement for the Thackeray Hotel, Lane's regular London base.

There had been an innocence about the reports of the opening years, lost when sex reared its head so openly in this garden. Rumours were flying. The community, because of the War and the resulting absence of older boys, and of the attempts at self-sufficiency, had turned claustrophobically inward. The Home Office committals, too, had contributed to the change in the atmosphere.

A big mistake, and one that was to tell seriously against Lane, was his preferential treatment of some of the girls. Ethel had been promoted to office work; it was even said that Lane was afraid of her. Annie Scott had been an early favourite, which had caused Ellen and Mary to be jealous. Annie had 'left in a huff' when she was replaced as favourite by Ellen.

In November 1916, Lane took Ellen, Mary and Cissie to the Grand Hotel in Torquay. The avowed purpose of this trip was to teach them 'how a boarding-house serves its meals'. 'I have always,' Lane later wrote, 'made it a point to provide changes or holidays for those citizens whose homes are such that they cannot visit them safely'. Cissie allegedly had a room adjoining Lane's, and was brought presents by him, again to the envy of Ellen and Mary.

Then Lane went on a second trip with the same girls, this time to London. He stayed at the Thackeray Hotel in Great Russell Street - his usual London haunt - with Cissie, while Ellen and Mary stayed overnight in Deptford. The reason Lane ultimately gave for this trip was that it allowed Ellen and Mary to see their parents, so they would not feel homesick and want to leave the Commonwealth prematurely. The Committee did nothing to stop this, they seldom interfered - though the trips were retrospectively deplored by Cecil Chapman in 1918 as Lane's 'American method of taking girls to hotels by way of a holiday treat'.

Again, in August 1917, Lane went off to Torquay with his daughter Cora, and with Ethel, Lizzie and Cissie. They spent their days in tents pitched on a site near Paignton. If Lane had not been there, the girls would have gone on holiday 'unattended'. He could not see why anyone should object to his arrangements. Any perceived 'impropriety...is a matter of convention', he said. Later, not everyone was to agree with this statement.

15
The Crisis

This atmosphere, the sense of there being 'something rotten' in the Commonwealth, came to a head in July 1917. Rumours abounded, quarrelling was endemic; Lane was biding his time - as he so often did - waiting for the crisis. At one Friday Court meeting, when there was so much squabbling that the Judge could not complete the session, he pointed out that self-government could not be continued under these conditions. He asked the citizens to tell him where the 'rotten spot' was. As it was by now late at night, the Chairman, William Jones, adjourned the meeting until Sunday. Bella and Ethel had to be compelled to attend. When they were accused of being the rotten spot, Ethel (Bella was silent throughout) was indignant, but said that she did know where the problem was. However, she refused to speak out until after the meeting, when she told Beth Jones that Lane had been having 'improper relations' with some of the girls.

Informed of this charge, Lane immediately reconvened the meeting, getting the citizens ('including some very bored boys') out of bed. When the meeting was told of the accusations there was an 'uproar of disapproval and indignation which was directed towards the girls from every quarter of the room'. Cissie and Minnie had to be restrained from attacking Ethel and Bella. Lane wrote, 'I was amazed at the situation, for it now appeared beyond doubt that there had been a quite general discussion among nearly all the citizens during the previous week about the insinuations made against myself'.

In fact Jane Bird, a graduate member of staff, had made similar accusations earlier in the month, at a meeting convened by the girls. Jane, 'popular, winsome and pretty' was noted for her untruthfulness - more kindly she was described as 'given to romancing'. She had been 'on the stage with a juvenile troupe' for eighteen months and probably enjoyed being the centre of attention once again. Jane later withdrew the charges, admitting that she had only wanted 'to make trouble'. She went home to Hartlepool, accompanied by Miss Bazeley, but came back to the Commonwealth of her own free will. Again, after working as a chambermaid for Lady Isabel Margesson at Barnt Green, she soon returned to the Commonwealth to work as chambermaid in Heather Cottage - and this despite her known dislike of 'soiling her hands'. Would she have returned if her accusations had any truth in them?

The Sunday meeting went on for two hours, during which Ethel and Bella still refused to state their charges openly. Ethel grew quieter, but Bella was in a state of mounting hysterical excitement. In the end, Lane suggested that they should go to Cerne Police Station in the morning and make their charges there, as they were such serious ones. The girls agreed, and Lane promised to take them.

But by the next morning, Lane had been taken ill. This has been regarded as suspicious, but he was already physically worn out by long hours of farmwork, and the meeting had exhausted him mentally. As he intended, it had cleared the air, but also left the two girls isolated. Lane was bitterly disappointed, and at this point seems to have had a brief breakdown.

Because of his collapse, the girls never informed the police. Nor did Lane inform his Committee. After about four days he recovered, and all seemed calm once more. So confident was he now that he took Ethel to stay at the Thackeray Hotel, to learn how to use a dictaphone and to discuss 'office details' with the Commonwealth's London accountant. Ethel, who was 'ambitious, keen and bright', had been doing a correspondence course in office work, prior to beginning a job in the Little Commonwealth's office. Lane explained that '[Ethel] had no suitable friend with whom she could stay in London, and I therefore secured a room for her at the hotel where I always stay when in London. She was in London two days attending to her work. On one evening I took her to a theatre, the Haymarket.'

He had then made the second trip to Torquay, which again included Ethel: '...the fact is that the unpleasantness of July did not occur to me as afffecting the inclusion of Ethel in this holiday party. One who knows the stress of emotion that prevails during adolescence does not visit permanent punishment and disapproval for hysterical actions, however serious may be their consequences.'

Lane never blamed anyone but himself for what happened in his life. He did not pass judgement on Ethel and Bella, though of course if he were in any way guilty he was in no position to do so. Nor did he make any effort to protect himself from blame. His shoulders were broad, and he took full responsibility upon them - which may explain his collapse after the crucial meeting.

Ethel and Bella remained isolated, and Lane realised that he should not have forced them to make a public statement. Commenting on the incident, M.L. Shaw of the Women's Training Colony at Newbury, acknowledged that such accusations are an occupational hazard ('all rescue workers are accused of immorality, male or female, by the girls if there is a loophole') but thought that Bella should have been appealed to on more personal grounds than citizenship - or else have been sent away. Shaw also thought (as did some of the Commonwealth's Committee) that Lane should have explained to the girls the possible outcome of their accusations. He should have consulted the other members of staff as well - if not the Committee.

In October the Executive Committee belatedly heard of the circumstances surrounding Iris McIntosh's departure. Three members of the Committee made enquiries in the Commonwealth. The trouble seemed to be over, and Bella, when interviewed, said it had all been 'nonsense'. Ivy's mother said she did not take the matter seriously and Bella's father was to say the same.

But Bella remained unpopular, and had not achieved her aim of being sent home. She absconded in mid-December, and was returned. On 30 December, 1917, she, with Minnie, Alfred Carr and Thomas Alfredson robbed the safe in the Commonwealth's office and ran away, separating once they had left the grounds. The boys were caught the next day and sent back to the Commonwealth. The two girls reached London, where they were at liberty for about a week before being arrested.

They made serious charges against Lane to the police, as Elsie Bazeley describes:

'[Bella] who had assured the Committee in October that her previous charges were untrue, and who a fortnight before had made no accusations against anyone in this same police court, now declared that Mr Lane had acted indecently towards her on two occasions. [Minnie], who in the previous July had most stoutly resented the charges brought by the other girls, now went further and stated that Mr Lane had had immoral connection with her.' They also accused him of behaving immorally with other girls.

As Lord Lytton was to note in his defence of Lane, these charges were becoming wilder: 'I can conceive that any man - even Mr Lane - might be led into a sinful relationship with one of the girls either by strong personal attachment or by a sudden and overwhelming temptation. But promiscuous misconduct of the kind suggested could only be committed by a man who was supersexual and morbidly unnatural. There are such men but Mr Lane is not one of them. If he were we should have to admit that he was also a super hypocrite, that his whole life was a lie and that all of us who have known him intimately for many years have been completely duped as to his character.'

Sure, confident, and intent on his work, Lane had at the same time a curious humility. He was not one to take advantage of any droit du seigneur, even one which was freely offered. The citizens - the girls, at least - called him 'Daddy' and he regarded them all as members of his family. They were children for whom he was responsible. At least some of the girls, prone to instability and hysteria, would have fantasised about this warm and attractive man, the only adult male permanently in the community, and competed jealously for his attention. If one girl claimed to have had 'relations' with him, then the others would not want to be left out. Hurling accusations was a part of the slangy, gossipy street life that they knew. Accuracy was not important to them. Nor was any concern for the consequences.

Lane was a man of action: his work was his life. Giving so generously of himself both emotionally and physically to others seemed to leave him with few inner resources. He had, at the very least, acted carelessly and with a disregard for propriety impossible to a man in his position. He acknowledged that 'Any degree of indelicacy on my part with any girl citizen would be sufficient cause for instant dismissal by my committee'. But as well as the trips he made with various girls, he also slept on the same landing as girls, whose doors were usually open. They took coffee to him in bed in the mornings. Lane's half-hearted attempts at self-defence against the charges were noted by more than one commentator. Lord Lytton wrote: 'No erring mortal or social misfit could wish for a better advocate, but whenever his own conduct or opinions were in question, he seemed to take an almost fiendish pleasure in misrepresenting himself and encouraging the mistaken opinion which others had formed of him.' And Miss Bazeley said, 'I think that he had extraordinarily little sense of self-preservation, but an equally extraordinary vitality and recuperative power.'

This latter power was soon to be tested. Cecil Chapman sent a telegram to Lane telling him of the whereabouts of the two girls, and asking Lane to collect them - but to be sure to visit him first. Chapman told Lane of the charges made against him, and that the Police had reported the matter to the Home Office. Lane had been summoned to a meeting.

16
Home Office Inquiry

Cecil Chapman accompanied Lane to the Home Office, where they and Lord Sandwich were interviewed by Sir Ernley Blackwell. Also present was Dr H.A.Norris, Charles Russell's successor as Chief Inspector. No full record was taken of this meeting, though notes on it survive. Dr Norris was silent but already, it seems, he was forming his own conclusions. The full story of the summer and of Bella's charges was told. Lane did not make a good impression, partly because of his native inability to act in his own defence, but mainly because of his claim that no accusations were made against him at the July meetings. This was technically true, as he had not seen the letters sent by Iris, Bella or Bertha to their parents, and the graver accusations of Ethel and Bella were not made to his face, but reported to him afterwards by Mrs Jones. Yet this claim undoubtedly sounded suspicious.

Lane then went on to a pre-arranged conference in Rugby. During his absence from the Commonwealth Dr Norris paid a visit, accompanied by his colleague, Mrs MacDougall. They interviewed some of the citizens. Norris was unmarried and forty two years old - the same age as Lane. He was a doctor of medicine who had specialised in public health. He began his career as an assistant school medical officer, after which he served with the Army in Gallipolli, Egypt and France. Norris comes across as rather a prurient man, hostile to Lane and to the Commonwealth. Unlike Russell, he had no previous experience of working with delinquents.

On 9 January, 1918, Mrs MacDougall interviewed Bella and Minnie, who were both being held in Southwark Workhouse. Bella told of how she had taken Lane's early morning coffee to his bedroom. She said that Lane had 'started feeling about my legs'. On a further occasion, she alleged, he had felt her breasts. He had also kissed her several times. And he had gone into Ethel's and Ellen's bedrooms at night. Minnie's accusations were even more serious. She claimed that Lane had 'behaved rudely to me on three occasions'. Both girls' accounts have the soft, unrealised touch of female adolescent fantasies. Minnie said '...he had on pyjamas - I was fully dressed - he lifted my clothes up, in front, and pulled down my knickers - they have an elastic band round the waist. I only said, "Don't Mr Lane". He was holding me on the bed - he loosened his pyjamas - he touched my private with his private - he put it into my private, he didn't hurt me much - then he was lying on top of me - he was moving up and down...' Minnie offered to be examined by a doctor, but no examination seems to have been made. Nor does anyone appear to have pointed out that Minnie had been sent to the Little Commonwealth for making similar kinds of accusation.

On 10 January, 1918, Lane was again interviewed by Blackwell, with Norris present. This was the first interview to be recorded. By this time it seems that the Home Office might already have come to a decision. Blackwell refused to give Lane permission to take Bella and Minnie back to the Commonwealth in his usual way with absconders. 'Being sent back to an institution of that kind seems to me and to the Home Secretary to be quite out of the question. It involves a question as to whether the Home Office will be unable to certify the institution.' It was a clash of personality and belief which was not advantageous to Lane. When he went on to Sandwich's house at Hinchingbrooke to meet members of the Committee, Cecil Chapman told him that Mrs MacDougall believed him to be guilty. The informality of the Little Commonwealth and the trips on which he had taken the girls told against him. Norris had recommended that the Commonwealth's certificate be withdrawn.

Lane therefore asked the Committee to demand a full inquiry and the General Committee, with Lord Lytton in the Chair, met on 15 January. Lane awaited the outcome of this meeting in another room. The General Committee passed a unanimous vote of confidence in Lane and a subcommittee consisting of Lytton, Sandwich, Hawker and Chapman was formed to investigate the matter further.

Obviously, the children were unsettled by events, and this in its turn upset Lane. He was further disturbed when he was refused admission to the Thackeray Hotel because Home Office officials had been investigating there. Lane wrote: 'I had been accused, tried, convicted and sentenced of unspeakable offences against decency without having been given any opportunity of defending myself against these accusations, or even of knowing what evidence had been placed before the Home Secretary.'

Nor was the Committee given time to carry out its own investigation. The Home Office decided to hold a private inquiry into the management of the Little Commonwealth and the charges made against its superintendent. J.F.P. Rawlinson, K.C., M.P., was asked to conduct it. This rapid response by the Home Office was thought by

David Wills to have been a bridling reaction to the 'pride of peers' who came so strongly to Lane's defence. Lane could not be tried in a magistrate's court because the girls involved were above the age of consent. But his fate would still be determined by a magistrate - a very well-qualified one: Rawlinson was Recorder of Cambridge, a county J.P. and the Unionist Member of Parliament for Cambridge University. Rawlinson and Norris, magistrate and plaintiff though they were, arrived together at the Commonwealth to investigate. They were there for forty-five minutes, during which time they examined the layout of the cottage bedrooms, even though the sleeping arrangements had been approved by the Home Office when Charles Russell was Chief Inspector. The two men did not talk to anyone, and Rawlinson refused to discuss the principles of the Commonwealth with Lane. His suspicions were aroused when some of the girls, who were washing their hands in the bathroom, suddenly bolted at the sound of the three men approaching. (He did not seem to know much about children.)

At Evershot station, where he had taken his visitors 'in the motor', Lane gave Rawlinson the paper he had prepared for the Committee. He was still being kept in the dark. 'Mr Rawlinson did not give me any information as to the form which he proposed to adopt in conducting his inquiry, nor did he make me acquainted with any of the details of the evidence that he may have had in the matter into which he proposed to inquire. I naturally expected that, since Dr Norris was with him and was to be present at the inquiry he (Dr Norris) would state during the progress of the inquiry the evidence he had gathered in the first investigation, in my presence, and that Mr Rawlinson would at the same time hear for the first time of the matter which he had been asked to judge...

'I had, in my own mind, looked upon the inquiry as an appeal from a decision that had been reached in the first investigation by Dr Norris or Sir Ernley Blackwell, and that the Home Secretary had asked Mr Rawlinson to represent him as the authority to whom appeals had been addressed. I had already been so impressed with the unfairness with which Dr Norris had submitted his recommendations condemning the Commonwealth to the Home Secretary without giving me a hearing or an opportunity for defence, that I felt it an indiscretion on his and Mr Rawlinson's part for them to be discussing the case before it came to the formal inquiry. I, of course, did not know that Mr Rawlinson had already had the whole of the evidence collected in the first investigation in his hands before the inquiry had commenced.'

To Lane's further disappointment, the next stage of the inquiry was held not at the Little Commonwealth, but at the Kings Arms Hotel in Dorchester. The only extant source for this part of the hearing is Lane himself. Lane went along with Elsie Bazeley, William Jones, Ethel Moore, Cissie Shorter and Jane Bird. As they were taking their seats, Ethel smiled or spoke to Cissie and Mr Rawlinson reproved them. 'Behave yourselves! This is a court!' Rawlinson went on to say that he thought a public trial, with members of the press present, would have been preferable. Lane, who was conducting his own defence, asked for the hearing to be adjourned until Lytton and Sandwich could be present. This request was refused.

William Jones then gave his evidence, which took more than two hours. He said he did not believe Bella and Minnie, and that the unwholesome atmosphere which had prevailed prior to the July meeting had cleared afterwards - and had not returned until Mr Norris's January visit. His statement referred to accusations of girls being 'fucked'. When Lane questioned William 'he said that it was not him that had used the word but Dr Norris. Dr Norris admitted this'.

Norris also introduced some new evidence concerning Lane's 'soiled linen', evidence on which Mr Rawlinson placed much emphasis. Lane wrote that, after the inquiry, Norris told him of Bella's claim that 'handkerchiefs had been found in my soiled linen with bloodstains on them. How had Mr Rawlinson obtained this information? And in what way was the matter relevant to the inquiry?'

Leslie and Cissie made confident witnesses. Jane Bird, however, became so frightened that she could not answer Rawlinson's questions. Lane commented: 'I then told Mr Rawlinson that [Jane] had never been considered wholly normal mentally, and advised that she be questioned more kindly if further facts were desired from her.'

Overnight, Lane put in writing his request for proceedings to be adjourned until Sandwich and Lytton could attend, and for future hearings to be held in London. Rawlinson again refused to agree. Lane persisted. 'I stated that the withdrawal of the certificate of the Commonwealth was the worst that could happen to me, irrespective of the findings of the inquiry concerning the charges of immorality against myself.'

Such obstinacy irritated the already unsympathetic Rawlinson. He seemed to think that Lane's objective in this request was to gain time, so that he could see Ethel's statement before it was used in the inquiry. Assisted by William and Ethel, Rawlinson examined the Commonwealth's papers, financial and otherwise, then finally adjourned the inquiry to London.

Hearings took place on seven more days between 8 February and 15 April, 1918. The report on the proceedings was never made public, and has since disappeared. Unusually, there is no trace of it in either the Public Record Office or in the Home Office Library. Lytton, Sandwich, Chapman and Hawker were present throughout. They remained convinced that Lane was innocent. But Lane refused to help himself, worsening the situation by the perverseness of his responses to Rawlinson. Bella had disappeared, and Lane's inability to find her was met with disbelief. He was on a treadmill between London and the hearings, and Dorset and the upheavals at the Commonwealth. Miss Bazeley, too, was often in London, and resigned from the Little Commonwealth shortly after the end of the inquiry.

Meanwhile, the Commonwealth was still accepting new citizens. Two children were admitted in the Spring of 1918, one of them a girl from Swansea called Katie Morgan, who arrived at the Commonwealth accompanied by her weeping mother. The only child of 'exceptionally honest' parents, she had 'nearly broken' their hearts by spending stolen money on sweets, and lying convincingly about it afterwards. She also claimed to have been attacked by a man, a phantom she described in great detail. She was, Lane commented, a very difficult case. He seemed to have no qualms about taking her on at this awkward time - and neither had the Home Office.

There was more absconding than usual. Lane told Sandwich that this was partly because 'the former effective measures' taken in the past could no longer be applied under Home Office rules. 'Spontaneous penalties' administered by citizens to other citizens included ducking and spanking. Lane had apparently made arrangements with Charles Russell when he was Chief Inspector to allow such unorthodox measures to continue. Now they had to stop. Otherwise, life went on more or less normally and Lane continued as best he could. The events of the past few months made no difference to his impartial attitude to the citizens. Then on 6 June, the letter from the Home Office arrived.

'My Lord,

I am directed by the Secretary of State to say that he has now received from Mr Rawlinson, K.C., his report on the inquiry as to the 'Little Commonwealth', and he regrets to inform the Committee that in view of the terms of the report it is impossible for him to continue the certificate of the 'Little Commonwealth' if it remains under the superintendence of Mr Homer Lane.

'If, however, the Committee will appoint another superintendent, and will make certain modifications in the arrangements and methods which will be indicated to them by the Chief Inspector of Reformatory and Industrial Schools, Sir George Cave will be glad to continue the certificate.'

I have the honour to be,
My Lord,
Your Lordship's obedient servant,
Edward Troup'

Addressed to the Earl of Sandwich, this letter was intercepted by Ethel in her role as office manager, as most of the other inquiry correspondence had been (much to Chief Inspector Norris's exasperation). The shocking news was broadcast by her to all the other citizens.

17
Closure

The Little Commonwealth Committee met on 14 June to discuss the situation. Lane, who had already said he would resign, was not present. But he was there at the next meeting on Friday 21 June, and read a statement in his own defence to the Committee. They were there, he said, 'due to a serious professional error on my part'. This 'error' was not the one that the Committee were expecting to discuss.

Lane was fighting for his professional life, so it seems only fair to quote his words at some length. He began by talking about Freud, and his theory of the Unconscious Mind: 'This hitherto unexplored region [which] is the laboratory of those instincts and feelings, physical, sensual, social and spiritual, out of which are developed the senses and perceptions which when conjoined with experience, produces consciousness of the Conscious Mind'. Freud had used his theory to alleviate 'mental diseases'; Lane noted the remarkable results that had been achieved by using Freud's methods in the treatment of shell shock. And now it emerged that Lane himself - and this must have come as a surprise to members of the Committee - had also been trying out some of Freud's theories. Using psychological approaches with delinquent children was a practice spreading in America, but in England it was still highly unusual.

'Now I have had the presumption to undertake to employ Freud's technique for the purposes of education, by a reverse process. He unravels the tangles in an unhappy and fruitless life, making the insane sane. I have tried to use his technique in education, in the building up of lives of joy and usefulness. He corrects insanity, I am trying to create sanity. He found that the great majority of his patients developed the symptoms of their several mental diseases during adolescence. It is obvious that in the treatment of my pupils I should find many evidences of mental abnormality, more or less developed, since I am dealing with persons well advanced in adolescence and who at the same time are delinquents. I must therefore use the Freudian technique in psychology in helping nearly every one of my pupils, in both directions, viz: to remove already formed obsessions and phobias from their paths, and then in a reverse process, re-educating and re-building. 'So far as I am aware', Lane continued, 'no other teacher has attempted to employ the Freudian methods systematically in any school...' Lane had been working as a pioneer and therefore felt able to state 'the premise upon which the technique of psycho-analysis rests for the purpose of practical application to education. The Freudian premise starts with creation hunger or, in his own terms, sexual hunger, and proceeds in a straight line through various forms of desire and craving to high ethical and moral ideals as the ultimate goal of life.'

Creation hunger, Lane said, 'being unaffected by our conscious moral or social concepts is unmoral - not immoral but unmoral. Freud designates this craving by the term 'libido'.' Lane went on to explain to the Committee how 'the content of the unconscious mind may be analysed, the libido brought out into the open, and its tremendous forces directed toward the service of the life-purposes of the individual and the welfare of society'. This could be achieved through the interpretation of dreams. Lane described how psychoanalysis could also be used successfully 'in the treatment of hysterical forms of physical ailments and in the relief of persons addicted to immoral habits, by a constructive process called "sublimation"'. For Lane, education was sublimation, 'pure and simple'. Or, put another way, Lane's interpretation of Freud saw life as potentially an upward spiral through cycles of instinct, consciousness and love. The 'ultimate goal' was reached with the love of God.

Lane went on to explain what he felt had gone wrong at the Little Commonwealth. 'The unhappy circumstances that brought about the necessity for this meeting today are the result of unconscious conflicts and sex perversities of citizens of the Commonwealth. One of my accusers is a pronounced sadist who has an obsessional fondness for

Charlie Chaplin and his brutal comedy; the other is a masochist. These two mental diseases are more prevalent in the Commonwealth than in any other community which I have known. It is not difficult to account for this in the light of psycho-analytic knowledge as follows:

'The conscious moral principles instilled deeply into the minds of the citizens of the Commonwealth by our form of self-government is so intense and so surely based upon logic and reason and experience that the libido which is definitely directed toward erotic or love objects, by the co-educational features of our school, must assume the deepest disguise in its power in order to evade the censor and affect the consciousness of the individual. Hence the prevalence of masochism or self-accusation in the Commonwealth.'

Such reactions paradoxically reaffirmed Lane's faith in the principles of the Commonwealth - because they showed them working. His error lay elsewhere, he explained.

'When, five years ago, I undertook the task of organizing the Commonwealth I was familiar to some extent with the theories and technique of psycho-analysis. I have always, up to a few weeks ago, felt a strong distaste for the responsibilities involved in making known to my pupils' conscious minds the fact of the transference of their libido to me as the "nearest parent". I knew that this transference was inevitable but I shrank from the responsibilities entailed by their consciousness of it. I devised a method of avoiding that responsibility that, until a few weeks ago, I sincerely believed in. The method was this: by allowing my pupils to create a community of their own, frame their own laws, administer their own courts, they being independent of their own parents' assistance through the wages scheme of the Commonwealth, I sought to secure transference from their own parents direct to their community without any intermediary in myself.'

This had not worked. Instead, many of the citizens, especially the girls, formed a transference-relationship to Lane. He had refused to accept this, and had therefore failed to deal with the consequences. In Freudian psychology, transference is the shifting of strong feelings from parent to analyst - and this, said Lane, was what had been happening at the Commonwealth. As a result, he had been forced to abandon his 'beautiful scheme' which he had hoped would serve as a model for other institutions.

'Mr Rawlinson has completely dissolved my complex. I now see clearly that the adolescent must still have a parent-substitute to accept his libido temporarily for purposes of dissolving complexes and conflicts, before that libido can be transferred to the community in which he lives...The adolescent is still a child.'

This was an oblique defence against some very serious charges. Lane must have been well aware of the effect his words would have on some of the members of the Committee - particularly his reference to Freud's idea that the basic instinct, even of a child, is sexual. Still more disturbing was the discovery that Lane had been putting some of these new theories into practice. On 24 June, Lane wrote to Miss Bazeley: 'The cat is out of the bag at last. I have now exposed my secret. All these years I have kept the real psychology of the Com. in the dark, but under the circumstances I felt that even though it might give the impression I was a presumptuous ass, I could no longer disguise the fact that I have for a long time been trying to out-Freud Freud...Of course the Committee are dreadfully excited about it and deeply prejudiced.'

Lane had probably come across Freud's ideas through G.Stanley Hall's *Adolescence*, published in 1905 and Ernest Jones's *Papers on Psycho-analysis* (1913). Though he did not mention it to the Committee, in the last few months, he had even been psychoanalysing some of the girls. One of them, Asena Oliver, wrote to Miss Bazeley in 1918, 'it is grand being sikeonaniquize bye and bye I will be able to tell the difference between right and wrong and make my whole mind work for me instead of 1/8 of it...' There is no evidence that he began doing this until after the Home Office inquiry. Thus it was most probably not one of the elements of the July 1917 crisis.

On 7 June [1917] Lane had written to tell George and Alberta Sandwich that he wanted to talk with them. 'I think I am on the scent of a great discovery re the psychology of the L.C. and the economics, religion etc...I am feeling that I have got hold of one or two of my more mistaken ideas re "personality" and influences and teaching, all affecting self-government and selfsupport etc.' Although the meaning of this is unclear, it may well relate to Lane's developing theories on psychoanalysis. It does show how dynamic his thought was regarding the Commonwealth. It also shows the closeness of Sandwich's involvement: Lane's declaration to the Committee of his 'new principles' could not have been new to him.

Lane's gamble worked. Amazed and uncomprehending as some Committee members must have been, they declared their complete faith in Lane, and agreed to continue the Commonwealth without Home Office support, as they had done before it was officially recognised in 1917.

But how? Otto Beit, Chairman of the Finance Committe, examined the Commonwealth's financial situation and by the time the main Committee met again on 2 July, it was immediately evident that they could not go on unaided. The Committee also feared that magistrates - and parents - would be reluctant to send children to the Commonwealth when informed of its parlous position. They already had difficulty in finding staff, and uncertainty about the future could only make matters worse.

Therefore the Committee reluctantly decided to close the Little Commonwealth for the duration of the War, hoping to re-open in peacetime with Lane as Superintendent. The draft statement notifying subscribers included the words 'unanimously agreed'. Lord Lytton, however, had not been present, and he still had to be consulted. This was no formality, as the Committee knew. On hearing of the decision, Lytton promptly resigned: he was not a man prepared to compromise. He wrote, 'I have a rooted conviction, partly justified by experience but in the main instinctive, that when an innocent person becomes involved in a scandal his only chance of escaping perpetual suffering if not actual ruin is to make a frank and full statement of all the facts which have produced the scandal and then to continue his normal existence exactly as before.' There should be no secrecy, whatever the consequences. 'In our case for instance if it be true, as some members of the Committee feel, that the public would not support us if they knew what had happened then our work cannot go on. We should not be justified in accepting support which was conditional upon ignorance of the crisis we have recently passed through. Probably all my colleagues will agree with me so far and that is why they have decided to close the Little Commonwealth for a time. The difference between us is that I am confident that by making a full statement of the facts we should win support, whereas they feel that we should lose it...'

38. Victor Bulwer-Lytton, second Earl of Lytton.

Lytton believed that Lane had not told the Committee of the happenings at the time of the July crisis because he did not think that they would understand. 'You are afraid that the public will misunderstand just as Lane was afraid we should misunderstand.' Disassociating himself from this stance, Lytton had no choice but to resign.

Men like Lytton and Sandwich would not have backed Lane if they had been in any doubt about his conduct towards the girls. But equally it was hardly surprising that some Committee members and supporters were mildly disillusioned by this point. Bertram Hawker, who attended the Home Office inquiry, was of the opinion that Rawlinson did not acquit Lane. Questions were asked about the state of Lane's marriage, about the fact that he and Mabel slept in different cottages. Although Lane had argued that for a well-integrated adult 'sexual abstinence [was] not only practicable but need bring no unhappiness' if that adult's energy was fully directed elsewhere, this might have been a difficult ideal for an attractive man in the prime of his life to achieve. Lane knew that Lady Sandwich had questioned some of his methods. She wrote to Lytton on 27 June, 1918 about Lane's preferential treatment of girls, who she claimed were '50% failures'. Yet despite these reservations she continued to regard Lane as an innocent genius.

There was yet another major concern. Lady Betty Balfour wrote to her brother Victor Lytton on 14 August,1918 that Lane was 'vastly careless about money...above and beyond his salary they had given him large presents - paid for the whole education of his children - and more than once cleared him of debt'. Financially at least, Lane was an embarrassment to his Committee.

The Committee decided that Lane should be paid until the end of September, and receive a gratuity of £200. Dr David offered him a post at Rugby School, which Lane did not feel he could accept. Lane returned to the Commonwealth to assist in the long, sad, complicated process of closure, and to help settle the children's futures. (The Home Office raised no objections to this.) There was a flurry of letters about the children. Citizens who had done well were released on licence. Some of the Montessori children had nowhere to go; the Home Office children were mainly returned to stricter regimes, though these were chosen carefully by Norris, Sandwich and Lane. Norris was willing to let suitable children stay working on the land (there was a severe shortage of agricultural labour). Lane recommended some boys for land work, and others for transfer to different schools. These recommendations were all followed by Norris. The boys were mostly sent to Sandbach Reformatory in Cheshire, 'where they do a lot of market gardening', and the girls to a new school at Huyton, Liverpool, run by the Salvation Army, which was, Sandwich wrote to Lane, the only school Norris 'could recommend for our girls'.

Three girls were transferred to the Homes of the Holy Redeemer at Duxhurst, near Reigate. These homes for inebriate women had been set up in 1895 by Lady Isabel Somerset, a dedicated temperance worker. Later a 'nest' for rescued children was added. Both women and children were treated with great kindness.

Meanwhile Ellen, who had left, returned in February to help during the last few months, filling part of the gap left by the departure of two adult housemothers. She loftily dismissed Bella's accusations as lies. Mabel Lane continued at the Commonwealth in her husband's absences while Raymond Lane was running the farm, assisted by some of the boys.

Homer Lane finally left the Little Commonwealth on 23 October, 1918, and moved to London with Mabel and their family. He also took with him two of the Montessori children; plus Cissie, who had no home and had been neglected by her father, 'a ticket man at the movies'; and Ellen, Jane and Ethel - the last two, of course being girls who had made charges against him. As ever, Lane bore no grudges against the citizens. He had worked on as usual during the last few melancholy months of the Commonwealth and his departure with the four girls brought forth no comment from the Home Office. This suggests that the prime purpose of the Rawlinson inquiry was to be rid of Lane as a controversial influence, and to close down an institution which a less radical inspector than Russell would never have approved at all.

Could the Commonwealth have continued without Lane? The Ford Republic had gone on without him and Lane himself always denied that he was an essential presence. 'In fact the Commonwealth runs itself. I am merely a citizen amongst citizens', he told the *Exeter Express and Echo*. If he were wrong, he said, then his system was a failure. But others doubted the Commonwealth's viability without him. Lady Betty Balfour suggested that the impression of democracy given by the Commonwealth was possibly deceptive. It could be that it was 'a one-man show', unable to proceed without Lane. In 1964, Lord Sandwich told David Wills that Lane was 'always on the spot' and never delegated. There was no one else at the Commonwealth who could have taken over his role.

Most experimental communities - therapeutic or artistic - have a figure-head with whom they are closely identified, and without whom they cannot long survive. One notable exception is Summerhill School, but for this there are exceptional reasons. Neill's daughter, Zoe Readhead, now in charge of Summerhill, says: 'I think it is because his methods were so well-established before he died and also because family, such as myself, were able to continue with the school. Having been a pupil here myself all of my school days was helpful'.

The Little Commonwealth did not reopen after the War. It was gone for ever. And one girl in particular scarcely survived its closure. Minnie, who left in the summer of 1918, wanted to return, if only to collect the brooch which Lane had given her for her birthday. Elsie Bazeley wrote: 'But there was no coming back for [Minnie]. The Commonwealth was closing, and that winter [Minnie] was caught in the influenza epidemic and was swept out beyond all human aid.'

18
A Wider Circle

And Lane? Despite his painful disappointment, Lane was still resilient enough to start all over again. He rented a rather grand house at 36 Highbury Hill, in North London, which was soon full of people. Ex-citizens came and went, or called in at the weekends. Ethel, Cissie and 'Croppy' (Jane) made themselves at home. A letter survives from Cissie in Herne Bay to 'Daddy' - a letter clearly expecting an indulgent response - asking if she can stay on holiday another week, before returning to the house. The Lanes also adopted Olive McLaughlin, one of the Montessori children. Feeding these extra mouths required more money than was readily available, and Mabel Lane had great difficulty in making ends meet. There were school fees too - Polly and Allan were sent to King Alfred's School in Hampstead, where A.S. Neill was now teaching. Lane gave talks on psychology to the staff which were not well-received. Neill wrote that Lane had sat 'with a face like vinegar' and afterwards declared that the school was full of hate.

39. Lane the psychotherapist.

Luckily for Lane, Lord Lytton arranged for him to give other more successful lectures. Initially, these were his main source of income, and some of them are collected in *Talks to Parents and Teachers*, published posthumously in 1928. (There was to have been a second volume of lectures published, but this never appeared, as the compilers failed to agree on Lane's methods as a pychotherapist. He was ever many things to different people.) Lane also became a 'consultant in psycho-analysis'. His methods were a 'Freudification' of the theories he had developed from his own practice and reading. They were not conventional, but he had no qualms about them. As he had said in his 1918 statement to the Little Commonwealth Committee about Freud's theory of the Unconscious Mind: 'This theory, being a theory only, one may adopt or modify as one perceives the truth in his own consciousness without affecting the technique of the science he has discovered'.

It was from Lane that A.S. Neill first heard this central theory of Freud's, during his fateful visit to the Commonwealth in 1917. He was among those analysed by Lane, along with Sandwich, Lytton, Lady Betty Balfour and Lady Constance Lytton. As he was not a qualified psychoanalyst, Lane called his patients pupils. He would do most of the talking, expounding Freud's theories, as he saw them, and analysing his pupils' dreams.

Neill had reservations about Lane's methods, but he was undoubtedly helped by them, as were nearly all his other pupils. Lane showed an amazing gift for empathy; the aetheistic Scottish dominie Neill, for example, could not have been more different from the patrician and deeply religious Lord Lytton, Governor of Bengal. Neill thought that Lane's big mistake was to work with adults instead of children, though Lane had little choice in the matter. It seems unlikely that he would have found Rugby School a congenial environment, and there were no other jobs on offer. He told Dr David that his reputation would do the school no good. So he continued to lecture to many different organisations, and he sought and found success as a therapist. His ideas became more Jungian, shifting from psychoanalysis to analytic psychology - partly because as a layman he could not call himself a psychoanalyst

Even Selfridges made use of his services. David Wills wrote that 'they had appointed as Director of Education and Staff Controller a very go-ahead young woman who knew Lane, and had been able to find jobs for some of the citizens. She had introduced a practice of having striking or provocative statements printed on the pay-packets, and then getting groups of employees together to discuss them. She got Lane to attend these discussions...' Lane suggested 'creating a community, self-governing, of the whole establishment. Install a children's dept. arranged chronologically to ages, manufacturing and distributing nursery apparatus (toys)...also a free cinema and scenic trips.' He was back on ground he knew and loved.

But still there were problems. Lane's methods had their dangers. His term for bringing out unconscious desires was 'undressing', which turned out to be an unfortunate one when the authorities once again had cause to check on him. As a therapist, he not only accepted - as he had to - the transference of loving feelings on to him, but also reciprocated - sometimes physically. As such transferences often involved a pupil offering gifts, Lane had no compunction about accepting them. He thought that this might help to heal the pupil. On the other hand, he did not insist on his fees if he thought a pupil was too poor to pay.

In the early 1920s Lane prospered. He had a house in the country and a consulting-room in Gordon Square, where two of his neighbours were the Bloomsbury psychoanalysts James and Alix Strachey (who, like many of Lane's more professional colleagues, regarded him with some suspicion). He was as extravagant and careless of himself as ever, and he was heading for his final downfall. The authorities had failed to rid themselves of him when the Little Commonwealth closed. Now, in 1924-25, they were about to try again.

One of Lane's pupils was a deeply neurotic young woman, whose family became worried by the number of gifts she was giving to him. These included money to pay his taxes and to buy a Sunbeam car. Lane was visited by the police, and charged with the technical offence of failing to register as an alien (another matter over which he had been careless). On his conviction, the prosecution brought up the events of July 1917 and recommended Lane's deportation as 'a dangerous charlatan and adventurer'.

A second, and very public trial began, steamily reported by the more sensational papers. It was alleged that 'French preventatives' had been found in Lane's London flat and 'indelicate watercolours' in his consulting-room. Further evidence was produced in a batch of letters sent to Lane by his pupil (and benefactor) 'Amy Nettleton'.

40. The last photograph.

Lane's barrister countered the accusations by claiming that the watercolours were donated by a grateful patient, and that the contraceptives had been left behind by others who had no need for them once they were successfully cured. As for the correspondence, since Amy Nettleton had at least once signed herself as 'God', they lacked any serious credibility.

Though some of his old supporters found this one charge too many, others of the great and good lined up to defend him. These included Dr

David, ex-Rugby School head who was now Bishop of Liverpool; the Revd H.H. Symonds, headmaster of Liverpool Institute; Lord Lytton, writing from India as Governor of Bengal; and his sister Lady Betty Balfour. Despite their testimonies, the magistrate sentenced Lane to a month's imprisonment after which he recommended deportation. During the resulting appeal, with a further array of defence witnesses, Lane made a deal: to avoid imprisonment and deportation he left the country voluntarily.

Four months later, Homer Lane was dead. He died of heart failure after typhoid and pneumonia on 5 September, 1925, in the American Hospital in Paris. Mabel was present, along with his daughter Polly and ex-citizen Jane Bird. Lane's body was cremated two days later in Père Lachaise Cemetery.

19
Some Citizens

What became of the citizens? Nothing is known of the fate of many, especially the boys who had enlisted. One boy went to India in 1918; others who had taken to the rural life continued in agricultural work as carters or labourers. Russell Blunt went to Preston Agricultural College. William Jones, who worked in a garage after leaving the Little Commonwealth, was injured in a motor-cycle accident, and was fitted with an artificial leg. He married, and found a job at Armstrong-Vickers. Ted Dalston, one of the first of the citizens, returned from the war and took a job with the Post Office. He kept in touch, grateful for the new direction his life had been given. Sam Tucker told David Wills that his Little Commonwealth years were the happiest of his life. After leaving the Army in 1918, he 'eventually joined a well known Police Force'. He then became an insurance claims inspector until his retirement.

Ethel Moore became Lane's daughter-in-law. Neither Homer nor Mabel Lane was pleased by this hastily-arranged match, which they feared would disrupt their son's career. A.S. Neill wrote: 'I recall the stern hateful face he had on when his son Raymond married the uneducated Ethel'. Raymond and Ethel were to have at least three children. Ethel was a good mother and a tireless knitter. Mabel Lane, maternal as she (fortunately) was, became reconciled to the union with the arrival of her grandchildren. Before her marriage, Ethel had worked at Selfridges where Lane had found her a place as student typist on the store's business scheme.

Cissie Shorter stayed for quite some while with the Lanes. She squabbled with Ethel, took various jobs, learnt Esparanto. Lane forbade her to walk out with the postman, but by 1927 she was reported to be happily married.

Jane Bird missed the Commonwealth after she left, sending wistful letters to Miss Bazeley from Lady Isabel Margesson's household. In 1927 she became pregnant, and had to go into a home for unmarried mothers, from where she continued to send some resolutely chirpy letters. Lady Betty Balfour helped her at this time, and Ethel supplied her with baby clothes. The baby was called Joyce Betty.

Bella Griffin was last glimpsed (by Ellen) at Deptford Fair, in the company of two soldiers and a girl of doubtful reputation named Hetty. She had returned to her work as leather-stitcher, and was a great frequenter of the Broadway Picture Palace in Deptford. Bella was definitely back in town.

And Ellen Stanley? - Ellen the wise judge, 'mother' to the small children who adored her, Ellen on whom Lane and Miss Bazeley came to depend. At the time of closure she told Miss Bazeley 'I simply hate to leave'. She got herself a job at the St Pancras Day Nursery, and afterwards worked as nursemaid to Max Plowman and his wife. Her letters to Miss Bazeley at this time - though misspelt - are confident and fluent. Afterwards she married a man called 'Joe' and had a baby boy. Her subsequent letters, written from various houses in the same Deptford street she had lived in as a child, are scrawled in pencil, sloping apologetically down the pages. One of them enclosed a pawn ticket which she asked Miss Bazeley to redeem. It was for her husband's suit, which he needed to start a new job on the railway at London Bridge.

Both Lane and Miss Bazeley helped Ellen financially at this difficult time. When her child was two years old, she found herself a job at the Macmillan Baby Camp. Ellen did not resort to theft, she had the resources and confidence to seek work, but she had to write begging letters out of desperation. She had slipped back into the poverty from which she had come, even to the very street from which she had been sent to the Commonwealth.

The 1920s were a time of high unemployment. In the winter of 1921-2 there were two million unemployed people in England and Wales. All the efforts of all the sympathetic magistrates and social workers, teachers and psychologists, were applying bandages to an untended wound. Poverty, material and emotional, was often the real criminal, and one which was extremely difficult to correct.

And yet - apart from some of the Home Office referrals - the citizens of the Little Commonwealth do not seem to have returned to their old ways. With Lane's help, they had broken the 'mind-forg'd manacles' of the slums. They had gained self-respect, and were able to make their own decisions, form lasting relationships. They kept in touch with one another, and with Homer Lane and Elsie Bazeley, preserving a sense of the family they had been for those five messy, disorderly, exhilarating years.

20
Disciples

Lawrence, Blake and Homer Lane, once healers in our English land;
These are dead as iron for ever; these can never hold our hand.

Lawrence was brought down by smut-hounds, Blake went dotty as he sang,
Homer Lane was killed in action by the Twickenham Baptist gang.

From 'Poem XXII' by W.H. Auden (*Poems* 1930)

W.H.Auden heard about Lane's life and ideas through his friend, John Layard, whom he had met in Berlin in 1928. Born in 1891, John Willoughby Layard read Medieval and Modern Languages at Cambridge. After graduating, he went in 1914-15 to conduct anthropological work on the island of Malekula in the New Hebrides (his book *Stone Men of Malekula* was published in 1942). His companion on this distant trip was the eminent psychologist W.H.R. Rivers, who later treated both Siegfried Sassoon and Wilfred Owen for shell shock. On his return from the New Hebrides, Layard suffered a severe nervous breakdown, resulting in physical paralysis, which Lane succeeded in curing. Physically sound, but still unable to write, Layard went after Lane's death to Vienna to find fresh psychiatric help. In 1926 he moved on to Berlin, where he was introduced to Auden by a mutual friend. W.H.R. Rivers was a link between them; he was revered by the poet's father, Dr George Auden.

Layard had been deeply impressed by Lane and was - though uncredited - the person who did most to prepare his uncollected writings for publication in 1928 as *Talks to Parents and Teachers*.

Layard also worked on the second, never-published volume. This must have been a painstaking labour, ordering and making sense of scattered, often ill-written typescripts, produced by a man so heedless of posterity.

Psychologically, Layard followed Lane's gradual move away from Freud's theories towards Jung's, and began to see patients of his own. His *The Lady of the Hare*, published in 1944, claimed to be the first book to describe the thoughts of an analyst and his reactions to the

41. Front cover illustration for *The Lady of the Hare.*

analysand. It is a study of the healing power of dreams (and, incidentally, a definitive account of the folklore of the hare).

Layard sometimes spoken harshly about Lane - he was in the middle of a negative transference to him at the time of Lane's death. He also thought that Lane did sleep with some of his women patients. But whatever he told Auden in the autumn of 1928 must have been enthralling: their first meeting lasted for hours, and Lane became for a while one of Auden's anti-authoritarian figureheads: huge, disreputable and unpredictable.

Auden was drawn to Lane's belief that human impulses are good, and that suppressing them leads only to mental and physical disease. In his notebook, Auden wrote: '"Be good and you will be happy" is a dangerous inversion. "Be happy and you will be good" is the truth.' Just a few weeks before he met Layard, Auden had probably been trying to curb his homosexual impulses - he spent three mysterious weeks in August 1928 with a psychologist in Belgium - but now in Berlin he intended to enjoy what the city and its bars had to offer. Layard, he wrote, 'fed/New doctrines into my receptive head'. Auden had known about Freud since his final school years -his father owned some of Freud's books - but Lane's theories suited him better, were more intoxicating. As Edward Mendelson has put it, 'Where Lane developed the romantic doctrine of man's original virtue, Freud pessimistically distrusted the violent and anarchic id... Where Freud hoped to do little more than reduce the sufferings of his patients to the ordinary misery of mankind, Lane promised happiness and freedom.' Thus Lane (mediated through Layard) became for a while a personal model for Auden, and a recurrent reference in his writings of the late 1920s and 1930s. Lane is the Bishop in *The Enemies of a Bishop*; he is there in Auden and MacNeice's *Letters from Iceland*, as late as 1937. But Auden's heroes were as transitory as Lane's own fame ('killed in action by the Twickenham Baptist Gang' as Auden mysteriously put it). One of Lane's most enduring disciples was A.S. Neill, as Neill was so often to acknowledge. In August 1920 he dedicated *A Dominie in Doubt* to him: truly a doubtful compliment. The book is a series of anecdotal ponderings on education, psychology and life in general. It faithfully records the homespun wisdom of Dauvit Todd the cobbler and other village worthies, in jokes as ponderous and whiskery as a old walrus. The dedication reads 'To Homer Lane, whose first lecture convinced me that I knew nothing about education. I owe much to him, but I hasten to warn educationalists that they must not hold him responsible for the views given in these pages. I never understood him fully enough to expound his wonderful educational theories.'

Neill's enduring monument is not his books - influential though some of them were - but Summerhill School. In 1921 Neill and Lilian Neustatter had founded the International School in Hellerau, Dresden, which was afterwards transferred to Sonntagsberg in Austria. Neill's first English school (1924-27) was based in a Georgian house called Summerhill in Lyme Regis, Dorset, where Neustatter's sister, the novelist Henry Handel Richardson and her husband George Robertson owned a second home. When the school moved to Leiston in Suffolk, its name remained unchanged. One of Summerhill's first pupils was Olive Lane, the Montessori child unofficially adopted by Mabel and Homer after the closure of the Little Commonwealth. On Lane's death she was informally re-adopted by Neill and Neustatter, and continued as a pupil at the school.

Neill received growing numbers of maladjusted middle-class children at Summerhill. Initially, his approach to treating them was mainly Freudian, with a further mix of Homer Lane, Alfred Adler and Wilhelm Stekel (whose patient he had been in Austria). Neill analysed children himself in what were known as 'private lessons', but found that 'most pupils cannot do much work with the man who is their father confessor', and so he abandoned this practice. He also moved away from Freud towards Wilhelm Reich.

Famously, children at Summerhill could choose not to attend classes. But they were expected to attend the weekly General School Meetings which collectively decided the community's laws. Neill's aim was to 'make the school fit the child' rather than the reverse - and more common - practice. His approach gradually came to influence the state school

42. The first Summerhill School, at Lyme Regis.

system, which moved away from its old, punishment-based, authoritarian attitudes towards a freer, more child-friendly environment.

The writer Ethel Mannin visited Neill's school in Lyme Regis. She had read his book *The Problem Child*, and was considering sending her five year old daughter to Summerhill. The house, now demolished, stood high above the town on the Charmouth road. A punctual visitor, Mannin walked across the 'untidy lawns' to the black and orange front door. 'I saw into a whitewashed hall with wildly futuristic paintings on the walls, and cocoanut matting on the stained boards of the floor'. The bell was - eventually - answered by a 'black-haired, stockingless, sandalled young woman' who turned out to be Olive Lane. There were more paintings in the living-room, a grand piano adorned with jam jars of wild flowers and 'rickety' shelves, overflowing with all kinds of books. There were no children to be seen: they had gone down to bathe in the sea.

This was Mannin's first encounter with Neill, whom she came to regard as a friend. Her novel, *Rose and Sylvie* (1938), is based on the true story of a servant girl (Rose) who ran away with a younger child (Sylvie), the daughter of her employers. Rose was charged with abduction, and in Mannin's story she is sent to 'Longmeadow', a colony for young delinquents. The superintendent is Roger Hollyback, 'the spiritual descendant of Homer Lane, that genius who believed that children are born good but made 'bad' by moral training, whose gospel of love was a gospel of approval...of whom it was said when he died that those who had known him were left with an abiding sensation that the world without him was not so safe as it had been, nor so sunny'. Ethel Mannin never visited Lane's 'gallant experiment', though she did correspond with Lord Lytton after the Commonwealth closed. In her portrait of Longmeadow, she attempted to 'convey the spirit, the Homer Lane-Neill attitude to what is known as delinquency'. Hollyback attends the Juvenile Court to select Rose, a child from a very poor, half-Gypsy home, for his community. The children are housed in family bungalows, which they have built for themselves. Although there are lessons in the morning, the emphasis is on manual labour. And Hollyback treats the children with unfailing love and understanding. Psychology is integral to his system, usually in the form of one-to-one talks with the child which are almost invariably successful, particularly in the case of Rose, who learns to overcome her fear of sexual love. Longmeadow is unmistakeably closer to the Little Commonwealth than to Summerhill (which Mannin had already described in *Green Willow* and in *Common-sense and the Child*).

Lane's other prominent disciple was his biographer, David Wills, who had discovered him through Miss Bazeley's book on the Little Commonwealth and through *Talks to Parents and Teachers*, both published in 1928. Wills' own elementary school education had not been happy - nor had his experiences as a 'brother' in a farm training colony. Keen to improve the lot of others, Wills qualified in America as a psychiatric social worker (the first Englishman to do so) and spent four years in adult education. Wills' encounter with the legacy of Homer Lane came at an opportune moment, because he had believed himself to be standing alone in the development of his thought on the treatment of problem children.

With a colleague, Wills drew up a plan for providing a therapeutic environment for problem children - particularly young offenders. This was published in the Quaker weekly, *The Friend*, in 1935. As a result of the article, Wills was contacted by the psychoanalyst Dr Marjorie Franklin, convenor of the Q Camps Committee. Q (Quest or Query) Camps had grown out of the Grith Pioneers, 'an experiment in creative living by unemployed men' (as the prospectus put it). These young pioneers acquired new skills by building wooden shelters out in the countryside, then running their own settlements. Q Camps worked on similar lines, but were aimed at young men less 'advanced in citizenship', including those on probation. A site was found at Great Bardfield in Essex, and Wills was appointed Chief of the new Hawkspur Camp. The Earl of Sandwich was a patron and the Little Commonwealth fund (see below, Chapter Twenty-one) donated £10.

Wills' book, *The Hawkspur Experiment*, was written in action. Like Bazeley's book on the Little Commonwealth, it is a lively evocation of a dynamic experiment. Conditions were basic, even uncomfortable; collective work was a part of the therapy. Wills himself, although qualified to do so, wisely refrained from any psychoanalysis of the boys. He was, he wrote, neither psychologist nor scientist. He was 'a Christian': a devout Quaker. Where necessary, psychoanalysis was done under the auspices of the Institute for the Scientific Treatment of Delinquency. A few boys made weekly visits to their London office. This did not prevent many transferences to Wills, both positive and negative. At Hawkspur he was at the centre of a 'vortex of emotion'. When one boy left he returned to Wills 'about thirty pencils, of all shapes, lengths and colours, from tiny bitten stumps to shiny full-length ones. "Here you are," he said, "I suppose you might as well have these back now." All these months, in order to re-assure himself, he had been stealing my love in the shape of its crudest symbol. Now he felt himself ready to get along without it.'

Although the Camp had a Council of boys who made decisions on everyday matters, the staff had the final say on more serious issues. The approach was one of shared responsibility rather than self-government. This enabled group members to contribute as much or as little as they felt able to do, placing less of a strain on often fragile young people. The system was a flexible one, and there was far less danger of its becoming static, as had happened with self-government at the Commonwealth in 1916. It also served as natural channel for group therapy.

Homer Lane was crucial to the development of this method. Although he would not have described his in this way, the meetings of his Citizens' Court were a highly effective form of group therapy. Participants had an equal voice and could air their views and grievances, discuss others' behaviour and hear their own discussed. Miss Bazeley wrote that any Little Commonwealth meeting was 'an occasion for searching group analysis'. Because the citizens shared family cottages, they also had other, more private, opportunities to express their feelings. Work, which brought its own satisfactions, was another therapy, as Lane himself seemed to find it, imbued as he was with that particular Protestant ethic. Work was at the centre of the Commonwealth's economic system, one to which the citizens had to contribute or else be a drain on their fellows. This involved the citizens in a shared responsibility. They were advanced ideas, especially when put into practice so comprehensively. The combination of Lane's vision, and Sandwich's necessary attention to detail, had created a unique community. Above all, there was Lane's unconditional love for the children, the first love some of them had ever been able to rely on. Love was the key. Wills' next venture - described in *The Barns Experiment* - involved a community of unbilletable evacuee boys in Peebleshire aged eight to fourteen. Here, shared responsibility was 'merely a corollary to our primary instrument - the instrument of love. First, foremost, and all the time the children must feel themselves to be loved.' This was not necessarily as easy as it sounds. 'It is not just a matter of being "awfully fond of children". Anyone can be that. It is a matter of being "awfully fond" of Johnny Jones whose table manners are nauseating (he sits opposite you and crams as much food into his mouth as he possibly can; this he chews with his big mouth wide open; presently he lets out a loud guffaw, ejecting his breath powerfully through his overful and open mouth...); it is a matter of being "awfully fond" of Willie Smith whose nose is usually in a condition such as to make one retch..' Work with boys like this was not for the sentimental. When Barns closed, Wills continued to engage with other experimental communities, but the Hawkspur Camp remains his most remarkable achievement. Merging together the very different experiences of Wills and Franklyn, it was the first practical experiment in Planned Environment Therapy.

David Wills' biography - his 'part payment' of his debt to Lane - was published in 1964. An extract appeared in the May 1964 edition of *Anarchy*, along with other articles on Lane by A.S. Neill, Anthony Weaver and 'John Ellerby' (*Anarchy's* editor, Colin Ward). This special issue inaugurated the new Homer Lane Society, which aimed to enable interested people to exchange ideas and experiences, and sponsor research and publications. 'Its primary objective, however, is to support the Homer Lane Trust in establishing a community for the treatment of emotionally and socially disturbed children.' The new community would develop the ideas and principles of David Wills. Though the Society fizzled out, the school was established, and the

Homer Lane Trust lasted until the late 1990s. (In the 1970s, at Wills' suggestion, the trust was merged with the Planned Environment Therapy Trust, with which it shared many aims and objectives. That Trust is still active today.)

A.S. Neill wrote that 'The tragedy of Lane's life was that he was associated with social scandal and not with the great work he did with problem children. In my early youth we knew Oscar Wilde as a bugger and not as a wit and dramatist. Scandal cannot kill a man's work forever, but it can during his lifetime.'

Lane has long been 'dead as iron', and his name almost forgotten - though oblivion would not have bothered him. Lane always lived very much in the present: lived almost for the moment. The future did not concern him. Yet - paradoxically - his ideas live on.

21
Hilfield Friary

Although the Little Commonwealth had gone forever, the Earl of Sandwich, undaunted, still wanted Flowers Farm to be used for altruistic purposes. A caretaker, Mr Hodge, was put into the building until September 1919, when the farm was leased to the Board of Agriculture and Fisheries as a farm for ex-soldiers. The project was managed by Dorset County Council, which was offered an option to purchase after three years. Instead, the Council gave up the lease early. Government funding was withdrawn, and the scheme had to be abandoned.

Sandwich then considered a religious community. Finally he offered Flowers Farm to Giles, a man who had lived and worked with wayfarers, sometimes resting from his travels with the Anglican Society of St John the Evangelist in Cowley, Oxford. When he was younger, Giles had entered the noviciate of the Franciscan Society of the Divine Compassion, leaving to follow an itinerant way of life. His ultimate aim was to found a religious community, devoted to the welfare of wayfarers. After the War, there were large numbers of ex-soldiers on the streets, some of them traumatised by their experiences, and as economic depression deepened, they were joined by growing numbers of other unemployed men.

Flowers Farm was leased to 'Edward Evans, known as Brother Giles, Friar' for seven years from September 29, 1921. The new community was originally called the Brotherhood of St Francis of Assissi in the Church of England. The Brothers planned to run an Industrial Home for Vagrants, who would work temporarily or permanently on the farm, 'in an environment which will help to revive or cultivate Christian tendencies'. Sandwich was chairman of the fund-raising committee, which soon resulted in him lending the Brotherhood £1,000. He must have felt a sense of *déjà vu*: finances were strained, Giles was exhausted by the farmwork (for which he had no training), the wayfarers came and went unpredictably. And as well as coping with these practicalities, Giles was also trying to form a religious community.

One day, Giles disappeared. According to the novelist Martin Boyd, who stayed at the farm soon afterwards, this was because of some minor sexual misdemeanour. The exact details were hushed up, but whatever they were, they proved unpardonable in those stricter days. Giles' accuser, Major Lloyd, was a man so strait-laced he once tried to obliterate the chalk phallus of the Giant of Cerne. In his memoir, *Day of My Delight*, Boyd describes how Major Lloyd accompanied Giles to the railway station and 'wept to see him go'.

Giles' unhappy departure left the community in a very precarious state. During his brief stewardship, however, he had managed to lay the foundations of the Friary, and to establish some of the traditions which are still observed, such as calling the wayfarers 'Brothers' and having the whole community eat their meals together: simple but significant parts of their everyday life.

His successor was Douglas Downes. Douglas shared Giles' sympathies with the poor, but at first he rejected the idea of creating a religious community even though Douglas, unlike Giles, was a priest.

Had Lord Sandwich not objected, he would have abandoned the Franciscan link. Under him, however, the community grew and its finances slowly improved, especially after the farm was given up around the end of 1924. Douglas was also firmer with the wayfarers. He began the practice of prayers after supper for all those who had ever lived in the community and for wayfarers on the roads. Brothers went out on missions, reporting on the often grim state of the overcrowded casual wards which provided vagrants with overnight accommodation, and actively campaigning for their reform. In 1928, they opened a new Franciscan home for wayfarers in Sherborne, the first of several such houses. Under Brother Algy, the Friary combined with the Brotherhood of the Love of Christ, becoming the First Order of the Society of Saint Francis.

The Friary continued to receive support from the Little Commonwealth Fund. In February 1921, what remained of the General Committee met to discuss the use of surplus funds from the sale of property and other profits accrued from closure. (Ten pounds was put aside to cover the costs of placing a Little Commonwealth girl who had 'got into trouble' in a maternity home.)

The Home of St Francis received an annual grant from the fund. The Committee felt it had a 'special claim', because it was on the site of the Commonwealth. In 1931 the fund paid for a telephone to be installed. Another beneficiary was Leila Rendel's Caldecott Community which - Lord Sandwich told Cecil Chapman in a letter of April 25, 1931 - was the 'only actual place which has developed upon the Little Commonwealth and Montessori lines'.

The Friary, too, began helping troubled children. In 1940, Veronica Cottage (by now rechristened Juniper) was used as a remand home for about fourteen boys between the ages of eight and seventeen. Within the community the boys were helped to rebuild their confidence and self-respect. Owen, who worked with the boys at the Friary, wanted to continue the work by starting a school for pre-adolescent delinquents. When he first came to the Friary, the wayfarers were mainly unemployed men between the ages of eighteen and thirty who were often maladjusted and of below average intelligence. Owen's experiences made him think that the Friary could most effectively help boys of a younger age group.

Owen found a suitable site, Hooke Court near Beaminster, which

43. Benchend in Hilfield Church:
'Suffer the Little Children to Come Unto Me'.

had once been the Dorset seat of the eighth Earl of Sandwich (Flowers Farm had been his shooting-lodge). The Ministry of Education advanced half the money, and the National Society lent the remainder.

Hooke Court was to become the first special school opened under the provisions of the 1944 Education Act, by which all children were to be given an education suited to their needs. The school was close enough to Beaminster for links to be established, and Owen encouraged these by holding open days and joining in local activities. He himself was a rural district councillor for over twenty years. Perhaps because of the remoteness of Flowers Farm, or because he saw its future as an independent unit, Lane had never tried to make similar links to the Little Commonwealth.

Hooke Court was a stately house; though conditions at the beginning were primitive. One woman teacher was provided with a room containing only a bed, a trunk and a candle. The privvy was on the wrong side of a bed of nettles. Mass was said daily, and staff and brothers soon became close under these challenging conditions. The boys, including six of the Juniper remand home boys who had not been transferred elsewhere, were divided into three houses according to age. There were practical and academic lessons and, where necessary, remedial teaching, but the school's essential aim was therapeutic. There were the usual, inevitable, problems with truancy, and to outsiders discipline seemed lax and conditions disordered. Like Lane, Owen was consistently on the side of the boys and relished their individuality. Owen was known as 'Father' Owen to the Hooke Court boys, just as Lane had been 'Daddy' to the citizens.

In her history of the Franciscans in Europe, *This Poor Sort*, Petà Dunstan writes of the school: 'The fact that the boys and staff worked, played and lived together meant this was a 'total community', one almost with a culture of its own, where pretence and subterfuge were well-nigh impossible. There had to be a shared vulnerability, a recognition that both boys and adults (parents as well as teachers) were 'damaged' in their different ways and it was the intensity of the shared life in which healing could take place for everyone.' Religion was a part of everyday life, and not imposed from the outside. At the same time, Owen's methods could be unconventional. He once sent an habitual truant on a hitch-hiking holiday with one of the Brothers; and gave a young thief an expensive present. When this gift was stolen, the boy experienced for himself the pain of losing a valued possession.

Owen's name will always be associated with the school. After he retired from the headship in 1966, he was succeeded by Brother Anselm, who spent time in a variety of teaching situations before taking over his duties. Great care was taken to ensure that the school could survive without its founder. Anselm made some changes, but St Francis School remained essentially the same. Father Owen suffered a stroke in 1976 and moved back to the Friary, where many of his former pupils came to visit him. He died in 1981. The school continued - after 1979 under a secular headmaster - until new regulations made it impossible to go on. Closure finally came in 1992.

Hilfield Friary, run by The Society of St Francis, has the serenity of a place at ease with itself. The old-style wayfarer has almost disappeared, but the Friary still accommodates young men in recovery from drug or alcohol addiction, from mental breakdown or other serious problems. The community goes on adapting to changing needs. Juniper House now caters for the carers, serving as a guesthouse for doctors, social workers and those nursing people at home. Thus the work of healing begun by Lane continues at the Friary to this day.

Appendix One

8, PORTMAN SQUARE,
LONDON, W.

Dear

As a result of a meeting held here rather more than a year ago, when a small Committee was formed with power to add to their number, to suggest a scheme for founding a self-governing community in England on the lines of the George Junior Republics in America, we, the undersigned, have now formed ourselves into an Executive Committee for that purpose.

Last year the Committee were so fortunate as to be given by the Earl of Sandwich the lease of a farm, rent free, in Dorsetshire, which will be available at Michaelmas next, and to obtain the services, as Superintendent, of Mr. Harold Large.

A Preliminary Fund was raised to enable him to visit the Republics in America, and to enquire into the problems, both psychological and administrative, that presented themselves. As a result of Mr. Large's report, the undertaking can now take definite shape.

GENERAL OBJECT.

The general object is to found self-governing communities for delinquent boys and girls who at the present time are either sent to a reformatory or an industrial school, or put on probation.

Voluntary cases will be accepted from parents or others in authority, of boys and girls who, although they may have eluded the police-court, are in reality indistinguishable in type from those who have come under its jurisdiction.

Though, as far as possible, admittance will not be refused to the physically unfit, it will be obviously impossible to include cases which come under the character of epileptic or feeble-minded.

THE GEORGE JUNIOR REPUBLICS AND THEIR METHODS.

The success of the methods adopted by the George Junior Republic is proved by the fact that since its inception fourteen years ago seven others have been started on similar lines; the promoters of the movement in England therefore are satisfied that the time is ripe for a similar effort to be made in the Mother-Country.

The principal results have been the formation of character, and the sense of citizenship acquired by the boys and girls at the Republics, and these qualities have been found to endure in after life.

This is due to the system, which contains elements totally different from those of any other attempting to deal with the same problems These are:-

(1.) Government by the citizens in all matters relating to the Republic itself, the laws being actually enacted by the citizens, based upon, and supplementary to the United States laws, with full judicial and executive powers.

(2.) A wage system, commensurate with the quality of the work performed, out of which a boy or girl pays for his or her maintenance.

Thus it will be seen that, with the solitary exception of the fact that there is always work available, the Republics are *an exact counterpart of the outside world*, while it is *a natural rather than an artificial community*, inasmuch as both sexes are included.

The immediate results of a self-governing and wage-earning system are:-

(1) To evoke enthusiasm on the side of law and order: -

(a) Because the initiation of rules and regulations lies with the citizens themselves, and they are not imposed by superior authority.

(b) Because, as soon as the citizens earn their wage they

at once exhibit the very natural desire for its security at the hands of the community, and therefore cease to have sympathy for the law-breaker.

(2) To introduce early into the life of a lawless child the maxim that "if any will not work, neither shall he eat."

As may be imagined, it not infrequently occurs that a new comer refuses to go to work, with the result that, even if he does no worse, he soon becomes a vagrant and a nuisance to the community; in this case he is prosecuted by the citizens themselves.

A SCHEME FOR ENGLAND.

The existing farmhouse will become the nucleus of what will ultimately be in appearance a small village.

Cottages, and the necessary buildings incidental to the life of the community will gradually be built, as the numbers increase, and funds allow.

It is considered that the maximum number of citizens in one community should not exceed eighty.

So far from attempting to copy American plans in detail, it is proposed, while retaining the fundamental principles necessary to the success of the scheme, *to adopt only those methods which harmonize with English life and English traditions*.

One of the essential elements for success is the grouping of the citizens in cottages in numbers sufficiently small to create the idea of home-life rather than barrack-life; under these conditions a boy or a girl has the best chance of becoming a personality rather than part of a machine.

Good school education will be provided in addition to farm work, and workshops will be built for teaching suitable trades. Both boys and girls will have equal opportunities of learning that which is most suitable to their capacity.

THE IDEAL.

The aim of the promoters will be first and foremost the training of individual character, to direct into good channels the natural energy which through bad environment or love of adventure has hitherto been misdirected, and, by means of the advantages of self-government coupled with a wage system, to create not only a sense of personal responsibility, but an appreciation of the value of membership in the community.

THE START.

It is proposed at the outset to begin operations with a very small number of citizens, realising that future success depends on a good start, and on the tone created in the initial stages.

The farmhouse, which is a modern building, is large and capable of holding some five adult helpers with about ten citizens.

The holding, like others in the vicinity, consists mostly of grass land suitable for dairy farming, but there are also some ten acres of good arable land.

As the numbers of the citizens increase, the conversion of some of the pasture into arable, allowed in the lease under certain conditions, will be effected, if it is found desirable to introduce intensive cultivation.

FINANCE.

The cost of the whole undertaking will be approximately as follows:-

<u>Capital</u>

A capital sum of £15,000 will be required for the cottages and other necessary buildings, including furnishing, stocking the farm, equipment, &c.

These figures have been arrived at after consultation with a well-known firm of architects.

MAINTENANCE.

After careful consideration it has been estimated that the annual cost of maintenance will be at the rate of approximately £50 per head, which for eighty citizens will amount to £4,000 a year. This is thought to be a reasonable estimate, considering the fact that a special staff is necessary for work of such exceptional nature, and that, under a wage system, provision must be made for a considerable margin over and above the actual cost of boarding and lodging the citizens.

A public meeting will be held in London in May, due notice of which will be given later, when a report on progress will be made.

You are invited to join in founding a society for the carrying out of the work and policy embodied in this letter.

Kindly state how many circulars may be sent to you for distribution among your friends.

Assistance is invited by:-

(1.) Donation.

(a) A sum down.

(b) A sum spread over a period of years.

(2.) Subscription.

(3.) Gifts in kind as the need arises.

We are, dear

Yours faithfully.

GEORGE MONTAGU (*Chairman*).
BERTRAM BROOKE.
CECIL CHAPMAN.
MARY ELCHO.
JANET JOHNSON.
PERCY MACHELL.
T. MOTT. OSBORNE.
ISABEL SOMERSET.
HAROLD LARGE (*Ex-Officio*).
EVELYN GREY.

Appendix Two

An undated extract (pages 19-23) from the typescript of Lord Lytton's 'An attempt to explain the principles of Lane's psychology'.

'So far I have taken only imaginary and hypothetical cases. Let me take Cissie's own case because it is that which I want you to understand and to help. She has an organic disease - valvular disease of the heart, a partly paralysed right arm and because of this heart trouble she has breathlessness and difficulty of speech which is greatly increased by any excitement. We know what is the matter with her. We know the immediate cause of her present condition. You and Dr. Barnes and Gerald and all "sensible people" *know* that this is no imaginary complaint - no mere hysteria - and are naturally disposed to question rather impatiently how this "silly dream business" can possibly do her any good. Now I have written all this down because I want you to understand that the process is not mysterious or spooky or supernatural - it has nothing to do with hypnotism, or suggestion or faith healing - it is absolutely and completely rational, logical and scientific. Above all it is not only not opposed to your own deep religious convictions but is the most complete vindication and exposition of the teachings of Christ. It does not depend upon any exceptional powers in the person of Lane - it works, if it works at all, absolutely automatically and unerringly in exactly the same way for everybody. The only uncertainty is the element of time, and that is where you can do a great deal to help or hinder by understanding or not understanding.

I have written at appalling length and have repeated things many times over because I am counting upon the effect of repetition to make you familiar with the process. I want you to be able to say when you have read this through several times: Well I do not really understand because I do not know any better than before *why* these things should be but I do at least partially understand *what* the process is, what is the part which dreams play in it, and what is the ultimate object.

Let me follow Cissie's case out so far as I know it up to the present. She goes to Lane and tells him that she does not dream. He replies . . . that she will do so and she does. Her first dream (I only know of this from a letter from Cis and she may not have reported accurately) was a most clear simple and concentrated presentation in symbolic form of the problem which I have described. She is sitting on a sofa talking to a clergyman - there comes a knock at the door, someone else asking to be admitted, the clergyman takes fright and disappears - there then enters an ugly man covered with earth and tries to take off her clothes. She wakes up in a fright. This is no doubt unintelligible to you as it was to her yet to me it seems so clear that I could not if I tried imagine any symbolism more exactly representing the situation in which everyone approaches analysis.

1. She is indoors - that means that the dream has to do with her inner life - not her vocational or outside interests.

2. She is on a sofa in conversation with a clergyman. The clergyman is a very obvious symbolism of what I have described as "mother law" - that is to say conventional morality learnt first from mother, nurse, governess and later upheld by religion, society, public opinion. He might have been a doctor or a policeman or a school-master, but a clergyman is the most obvious and the most complete personification of this authority because he represents religion as well as public opinion. Cissie having accepted the authority of "mother law" (the clergyman) is quite comfortable and happy with him until the knock on the door recalls "mother nature" with whom the clergyman is not on speaking terms, but she is on a sofa, that is, an invalid - an absolutely perfect representation of her present condition.

3. Then comes the knock at the door and the clergyman takes fright, naturally because "mother law" and "mother nature" cannot meet. The door is the door of analysis through which "mother nature" gains admittance - but because she has accepted the teaching of the clergyman "mother nature" (that is Cis's own personality at birth, her untutored conscience with all its race instincts and impulses) is represented as a hideous and terrible enemy "covered with earth" to contrast the place he comes from with the heaven of the clergyman.

4. The first thing he does is to say "strip off those clothes". Clothes in dreams symbolise acquired thoughts or protection. This is of course what mother nature wants Cis to do - divest herself of all the teachings of the clergyman, the "clothes" with which she has covered up her naked soul to protect it from the criticisms of the world.

If she could have stood up in her dream and having divested herself of all her clothes turned to the ugly earth-man and said "see now I am fair embrace me" she would have woken up cured, because that would have meant reconciliation with her disapproved and suppressed unconscious, but that was not possible for the clergyman would be shocked. She is afraid of the earth-man, she is afraid of the nakedness which in dream symbolism means truth and therefore she wakes up in a sweat of fear.

Now the interpretation of the dream to Cissie will do her no good. It will merely be an amusing intellectual game . . . She will have to dream many more dreams in which that same clergyman and earth-man will appear in countless disguises before she even realises herself what they represent. The next thing that will happen will be an admission that in spite of her life long efforts to keep this earth-man shut out behind the door he will at times intrude and that his intrusions are most unwelcome - that will be a difficult and unhappy time. Finally she will come to know that this earth-man is in reality the divine part of her own soul - an Angel of God not to be hated and despised and kept outside the door but to be welcomed and encouraged. He will then be introduced to the clergyman, the two will be reconciled and embrace and Cissie will be cured.'

Appendix Three

GIRLS' REFORMATORY AND INDUSTRIAL SCHOOLS

Rules as to Punishment

1. The Superintendent shall use every endeavour to reduce all forms of punishment to the minimum compatible with the welfare of the children and of the School.

2. Punishments shall consist of

(a) Forfeiture of privileges or rewards, loss of marks, loss of playtime, deprivation of liberty, &c., or degradation in rank.

(b) Alteration of diet.

(c) For children over 12 separate confinement in a light and airy room.

(d) In exceptional circumstances light and moderate corporal punishment.

As regards (a) care shall be taken that no girl shall be deprived of recreation to an extent which would be injurious to health.

As regards (b) a girl may be deprived of that portion of a meal which renders it most agreeable, but the nutritive value of the meal shall not be substantially diminished.

As regards (c) no girl under 12 shall be punished by separate confinement.

No girl over 12 and under 14 shall be confined separately for a longer period than 24 hours.

No girl over 14 shall be confined separately for a longer period than 48 hours, except with the consent of one of the Managers of the

School. Any case of confinement for more than 48 hours with such consent shall be reported immediately with an explanation of the circumstances to the Chief Inspector.

No girl shall be kept in separate confinement in darkness.

If a girl is confined separately for more than 12 hours, some form of occupation shall be provided for her.

As regards (d), the discretion of the Superintendent to inflict in exceptional circumstances some light and moderate corporal punishment, shall be exercised only as a last resort, and when all other methods of maintaining discipline have failed.

Such punishment shall only be inflicted by the Superintendent, or in her presence and under her direction.

No such punishment shall be inflicted in the presence of other girls.

Every such punishment shall be reported to the Managers at their next meeting, and a full explanation given to them of the method of punishment and the reasons for its infliction.

3. Except as provided in Rule 2 no person employed in the School shall inflict any kind of corporal punishment and the term "corporal punishment" includes any form of striking, cuffing, shaking, or physical violence.

If any person employed in the School is found breaking this rule, the Superintendent shall report the case to the Managers.

The Superintendent shall bring this rule to the notice of every person employed in the School.

4. The Superintendent shall be responsible for seeing that (a) all corporal punishments, (b) all punishments by solitary confinement, (c) all other serious punishments, and (d) any general punishments inflicted on the whole School or the whole of any class or division, are recorded without delay in one Punishment Book.

This book shall show

(a) the date of the punishment;

(b) the name of the offender;

(c) her age;

(d) the nature of the offence;

(e) the name of the officer reporting the girl for punishment;
(f) the method and degree of the punishment.

5. The Punishment Book shall be examined at each meeting of the Managers and initialled by the Chairman of the meeting.

Home Office, Whitehall.
1st September, 1915.

Bibliography

PRIMARY SOURCES

1 Published

Bazeley, E.T, *Homer Lane and the Little Commonwealth*. London, Allen & Unwin, 1928.
Bridgeland, Maurice, *Pioneer Work with Maladjusted Children*. London, Staples Press, 1971.
Wills, W. David, *Homer Lane: a Biography*. London, Allen & Unwin, 1964.

2 Unpublished

Dorset Record Office, Dorchester, Dorset. D/LCW. An extensive archive of manuscripts, ledgers, typescripts, letters, notes, pamphlets, catalogues, plans and press-cuttings relating to the Little Commonwealth, of which the most relevant are listed below:

1/1 Signed minutes of the General Committee. Includes a letter from the Committee to the Home Office 9 Jul 1918, a letter of resignation from Lord Lytton 6 Jul 1918, and draft letters to parents and subscribers about the closure. One vol, Jul 1913 - Jun 1925.
2/3/1 Distribution of expenses. Details of housekeeping, mechanical, farm livestock, farm crops, educational, executive, social, buildings and housing, religious, citizens and industrial accounts for each month. One vol, Jul 1913 - Sep 1918.
2/3/2 Details of expenses, housing and food costs; income and statistical information by week for the cottages Bramble, Heather and Bracken. One vol, May 1914 - Sep 1918.
2/4/1 Cash book (receipts and expenditure). One vol, Aug 1911 - Oct 1924.
2/4/2 Secondary accounts. Journal. One vol, Jun 1913- May 1922.
2/5/1 Building Fund. Receipts. One vol, Jul 1914 - Feb 1916.
2/6/1 Ledger of subscriptions paid by sponsoring authorities and private guardians for citizens. One vol, Sep 1917- Sep 1918.

2/7/1 Accounts of expenses incurred by Mr Lane and other members of staff and citizens in attending the Home Office enquiry. One doc, 26 Apr 1918.
2/8/1 Correspondence and receipts relating to the establishment and financial administration of the Little Commonwealth Fund; donations mainly to the Home of St Francis and the Caldecott Community. 69 docs, Jan 1921 - Aug 1935.
2/8/2 File containing receipts for war bonds; income tax claim account; list of citizens in residence at 30 Jun 1918; two letters from Lord Sandwich about the establishment of the St Francis Home. 7 docs, c.Sep 1918 - Jan 1922.
2/8/3 Correspondence relating to citizens killed in the First World War and the erection of a war memorial in Batcombe Church. 5 docs, Nov - Dec 1922.
2/8/4 Correspondence between Lord Sandwich, committee members and the Bishop of Liverpool about a donation to Mrs Lane after the death of Homer Lane, 1925; the placing of a memorial to him at the Little Commonwealth and the publication of books based on his work; articles from *The Times* about a court case involving Homer Lane 1925; correspondence between Lady Sandwich and Mrs Lane about Homer Lane's death and the family, 1925, 1929; letter from Raymond Lane about a former citizen 1926; fund accounts 1926. 51 docs, Mar 1925 - Jan 1929.
2/8/5 Correspondence with Lord Sandwich relating to the establishment and funding of Q Camps including printed reports. 27 docs, May 1935 - Jun 1936.
2/8/6 Correspondence and receipts relating to donations mainly to Q Camps and the Home of St Francis. Includes a copy of the constitution of the Little Commonwealth. 50 docs, Jul 1935 - Jul 1940.
3/1/1 Copy out-letters from George Montagu to Homer Lane. One vol, 13 Oct 1915 - 30 Jan 1916.
3/1/2 Copy out-letters from George Montagu to correspondents, 13 Oct 1915 - 15 Feb 1916, and to Lane, 1 Feb 1916 - 10 Feb 1916. One vol.
3/1/3 In-letters concerning subscriptions and donations, citizens, visits to the Little Commonwealth and equipment 376 docs, Aug 1916 - May 1920.
3/2/1 Correspondence to and from Homer Lane relating to the admission, discharge and absconding of various citizens and details of citizens' claims and maintenance payments. Jun 1917. 4 docs. Apr 1917 - Feb 1918.
3/3/1 Correspondence from Homer Lane and others mainly to Lord Sandwich relating to the closure of the Little Commonweath. Includes a draft letter to the parents of citizens, an official letter to subscribers and a copy letter of resignation of the school's certificate to the Home Office. 105 pieces.. Jan 1918 - Oct 1918.
3/3/2 Printed account by Homer Lane of events entitled *The Closing of the Little Commonwealth* issued by the Committee, statement to subscribers and rough drafts and notes. 9 docs n.d. [1918/1919].
3/3/3 Notes on the Home Office enquiry, including Mr Lane's account of the investigation. One doc. n.d. [1918].
3/3/4 Paper presented to the General Committee 22 Jun 1918 by Mr Lane explaining the Freudian principles on which the Little Commonwealth was based. One doc.

1918.
3/3/5 Rough transcript of a statement by Mrs Jones of events at the Little Commonwealth One doc. 20, 22 Jan [?1918].
3/3/6 Rough notes of events at the Citizens Court, summer I917. 8 pieces n d. [c? 1918].
3/3/7 Notes and comments on the statements of various people during the enquiry, notes for an official statement by Lord Sandwich, and notes on the funding of the Little Commonwealth. 40 pieces n.d. [?1918].
5/1 Second Annual Report 1914-1915 Includes a summary of the laws and principles of the Little Commonwealth. Block plan and photographs of the cottages, balance sheet at 30 Jun 1915 and income and expenditure account I Jul 1914 - 30 Jun 1915. One booklet 1915.
5/2 Third Annual Report 1915 - 1916. Includes balance sheet as at 30 Jun 1916 and income and expenditure account 1 Jul 1915 - 30 Jun 1916. One booklet 1916.
6/1 Probation Officer's Record Book. Gives citizens' case histories sometimes with details after they left the Little Commonwealth. One vol. Jun 1915 - Sep 1918.
6/2 Register of citizens' medical records. One vol. May- Dec 1917.
6/3 Letter from Lord Sandwich to Homer Lane, discussing the procedure for transferring citizens from the Little Commonwealth to schools or employment. One doc. 19 Jul 1918.
6/4 Reports on the character of citizens and recommendations as to their transfer to other schools or employment. 30 docs. n.d. [1918].
7/l/1 Elevations, sections and floor plans [of Bracken Cottage]. n.d. [c. 1913].
7/1/2 Elevations, sections and floor plans of proposed cottage [Heather Cottage] n.d. [c 1913].
7/2/1 Bramble Cottage housekeeping furnishings Contains an inventory of equipment and furniture Jul 1915 - Sep 1916; work lists Jul - Aug? 1915/1916; inventory of personal articles in various rooms Dec 1915 - Jul 1916. One vol.
8/1/1 Rules of the Little Commonwealth. 25 pieces, 1915.
8/1/2 Register of the Children's Court. One vol. Dec 1913 - Nov 1917.
8/3/1 Dairy account book. Contains an inventory of cows and equipment and daily summary of milk yields for July. One vol, Jul - Sep 1918.
9/1/1 Articles from national, local and international newspapers about the foundation and progress of The Little Commonwealth Jan 1911 - May 1914, with some loose cuttings about the closure, 1918. One vol.
9/1/2 Articles mainly from local newspapers about the foundation of the Little Commonwealth. One vol, May 1912 - Jun 1912.
9/2/1 Home Office rules for girls' reformatory and industrial schools. One doc, 1915.
10/1 Catalogue of the sale of farm stock and equipment of the Little Comrnonwealth held on 25 Mar 1919. 2 docs, 1919.
10/3 Catalogue of the sale of scientific and photographic apparatus held on 25 Jul 1919 including some equipment from the Little Commonwealth.

11/1 Descriptions of the home for vagrants including details of the staff and meals provided. Two docs n.d. [1921, 1922].
11/2 Correspondence and receipts relating to donations from the Little Commonwealth Fund to the brotherhood. 14 docs, Jun 1923 - Jun 1924.

Planned Environment Therpy Trust, Toddington, Cheltenham
PP/WDW. Comprehensive David Wills Collection, including his research material for *Homer Lane: a Biography*. Particularly useful for Lane's early life before leaving America and for interviews made by Wills with Lord Sandwich, Bertram Hawker, J.H. Simpson and Cora Lane. Also containing some of E.T.Bazeley's notes for *Homer Lane and the Little Commonwealth*, and letters to her from citizens, both during the Commonwealth and after its closure.

Knebworth House Archive, Old Knebworth, Herts
Three boxes of uncatalogued papers belonging to Lord Victor Lytton. Boxes I and 2 include letters relating to events leading to the closure of the Little Commonwealth, 1918 -19 and assessments of Lane's culpability. Letters from Lady Sandwich, Lady Betty Balfour. Notes by Lord Lytton contesting the Home Office verdict and his own version of the Report on the closure of the Little Commonwealth. Some letters from citizens.
Box 3 includes Lytton's 'An attempt to explain the principles of Lane's psychology' (n.d.).

Warwick Modern Records Centre
MSS.16c/3/LC/1 First Annual Report of the Little Commonwealth, 1914.
MSS.I6c/3/LC/6 'Some unsolicited Impressions of the Little Commonwealth', reprinted from *Exeter Express and Echo* [1916].
MSS.16c/3/LC/8 Notes by Dr H. Wilson, Chairman of the managers of Newbury Women's Training Colony, concerning the closure of the Little Commonwealth, 1918.
MSS.16c/3/LC/9 Letter to Dr Wilson from M.L. Shaw, concerning the closure.
MSS.16c/5/1/16 Report on the Closure of Riverside Village [1917].

Dorset County Museum, Dorchester, Dorset.
Photocopies of the first and last pages of the Little Commonwealth Visitors' Book.
Hardy, Thomas. Draft letter to the editor *Notes and Queries*, concerning the Cross-in-Hand, undated.
Moule, Henry Joseph. Letter to Emma Hardy, Michaelmas 1900.

Other Sources
Conversations with Craig Fees of PETT, Brother Philip Bartholomew and Brother Reginald of Hilfield Friary.

Correspondence with Bryn Purdy, Colin Ward and Zoe Readhead.
'Prophets, Charlatans and Little Gurus'. Discussion on Homer Lane with Ray Gosling, Harry Thompson, Kenneth Barnes and Colin Ward. Produced by Alistair Wilson, Radio 4, Nov. 14, 1982.
'Undesirable Alien'. Play about Homer Lane by Allen Saddler. Radio 4, 1982.

SECONDARY SOURCES

I Published

Auden,W.H. & MacNeice, Louis, *Letters From Iceland*. London, Faber & Faber, 1937.
Auden, W. H., *Poems*. London, Faber & Faber, 1930.
Balsan, Consuelo Vanderbilt, *The Glitter and the Gold*. London, Heinemann, 1953.
Blishen, Edward, (ed.), *Blond's Encyclopaedia of Education*. London, Blond Educational, 1969.
Boyd, Martin, *Day of My Delight*. Melbourne & London, Lansdowne Press, 1965.
The Builder, Obituary of C.H. Biddulph-Pinchard. May 19, 1944.
Burt, Cyril, *The Young Delinquent*. London, University of London Press, 1925.
Carpenter, Humphrey, *W.H. Auden: a biography*. London, Allen & Unwin, 1981.
Chaplin, Charles, *My Autobiography*. London, Bodley Head, 1964.
Chapman, Cecil, *The Poor Man's Justice*. London, Hodder & Stoughton, [1925].
Coffin, Leslie W., *Cerne Abbas & Villages*. Holnest, Sherborne, Miss S.E.M. Coffin, [1987].
Croall, Jonathan, (ed.), *All the Best, Neill*. London, Andre Deutsch, 1983.
Croall, Jonathan, *Neill of Summerhill: the permanent rebel*. London, Routledge & Kegan Paul, 1983.
Darton, F.J. Harvey, *The Marches of Wessex*. London, Newnes, 1922.
Dictionary of National Biography.
Dorset County Chronicle, July 31, 1913; Nov 27, 1913.
Dunstan, Petà, *This Poor Sort*. London, Darton, Longman and Todd, 1997.
Evans, George Ewart & Thomson, David, *The Leaping Hare*. London, Faber & Faber, 1972.
Hardy, Thomas, *Poems of the Past and Present*. London, Harper & Bros, 1902 [1901].
Hardy Thomas. *The Woodlanders*. London, Macmillan, 1887.
Headquarters Gazette, September 1911, July 1912, February 1914, March 1916.
Hilfield and Hermitage Women's Institute, *Village Record of Hermitage and Hilfield*, 1965.
Hoare F.R. 'Principles of Discipline and Self-government. An experiment at Riverside Village'. Report of the Sixth Annual Conference of Educational Associations, 1918.
Holmes, Thomas, *The London Police Courts*. London, Nelson. n.d. [190?].

Jones, Howard, *Reluctant Rebels*. London, Tavistock, 1960.
Judge, Roy, 'Mary Neal and the Espérance Morris'. *Folk Music Journal*, Vol. 5, No 5. London, English Folk Dance & Song Society, 1989.
Kelly's Directory of Dorsetshire, 1915.
Kerr, Barbara, *Bound to the Soil*. London, John Baker, 1968.
Lane, Homer, *Talks to Parents and Teachers*. London, Allen & Unwin, 1928.
Layard, John, *The Lady of the Hare*. London, Faber & Faber, 1944.
Low, Barbara, ' The Little Commonwealth', *School Hygiene,* 1916.
Lytton, Earl of, *New Treasure. A Study of the Psychology of Love*. London, Allen & Unwin, 1934.
MacMunn,Norman *A Path to Freedom in the School*. London, Curwen & Sons, 1914.
Mannin, Ethel, *Confessions and Impressions*. London, Penguin, 1937.
Mannin, Ethel, *Green Willow*. London, Hutchinson, n.d.
Mannin, Ethel, *Rose and Sylvie*. London, Jarrolds, n.d. [1938?].
Marlow, Joyce, *The Tolpuddle Martyrs*. London, Deutsch, 1971.
Mayhew, Henry, (edited by Peter Quennell), *Mayhew's London*..London, Spring Books, 1969.
Meisel, Perry and Kendrick, Walter, *Bloomsbury/Freud: The Letters of James and Alix Strachey 1924-1925*. London, Chatto & Windus, 1986.
Mendelson, Edward, *Early Auden*. London, Faber & Faber, revised and corrected edition, 1999.
Montessori, Maria, *Dr Montessori's Own Handbook*. New York, Schocken Books, 1965.
Neill, A S, *A Dominie in Doubt*. London, Herbert Jenkins, [1921].
Neill, A S, *A Dominie's Log*. London, Herbert Jenkins, 1915.
Neill, A S, *'Neill, Neill, Orange Peel!'* London, Weidenfeld & Nicolson, 1973.
Neill, A S, *That Dreadful School*. London, Herbert Jenkins, 1937.
Neill, A S, *Summerhill*. London, Gollancz, 1962.
Penal Reform League Quarterly Record. Vol V1, No I, Jan 1914.
Perry, Leslie R., *Bertrand Russell/A.S.Neill/Homer Lane/W.H.Kirkpatrick,* Collier-Macmillan, 1967.
Potter, Cecil, 'The Scout Farm'. *The Scouter*, September 1960.
Pound, Reginald, *Selfridge*. London, Heinemann, 1960.
Richman, Geoff, *Fly a Flag for Poplar*. London, Liberation Films, [1974].
Russell, Bertrand, *Autobiography* Vol. 2, London, Allen & Unwin, 1968.
Simpson, J.H. *An Adventure in Education*. London, Sidgwick & Jackson, 1929.
Simpson, J.H. *Sane Schooling*. London, Faber & Faber, 1936.
Simpson, J.H. *Schoolmaster's Harvest*. London, Faber & Faber, 1954.
Somerset & Dorset Notes and Queries, Vol.1, 1890; Vol.11, 1891.
Standing, E.M. *Maria Montessori, Her Life and Work,* Hollis & Carter, 1957.
Stevenson, John, British Society 1914-45. Harmondsworth, Penguin, 1954.
Udal, John Symonds, *Dorsetshire Folk-lore*. Hertford, Stephen Austin, 1922.

Ward, Colin, (ed.), 'The Legacy of Homer Lane'. *Anarchy* 39. London, Freedom Press, May 1964.
Waring, Edward, *Ghosts and Legends of the English Countryside*. Tisbury, Compton Press, 1977.
Who Was Who, 1961-1970.
Wills, W. David, *The Barns Experiment*. London, Allen & Unwin, 1945.
Wills, W. David, *The Hawkspur Experiment*. London, Allen & Unwin, 1941.
Woods, Alice, *Advance in Co-education*, with an introduction by Homer Lane. London, Sidgwick & Jackson, 1919.